THE WI
CAKES

LYN MANN

WI BOOKS

ACKNOWLEDGEMENTS

The author would like to thank Dawn Clarke, Eileen Henson, Lyn Lorenc and Sara Staker for their unending patience in the testing and evaluation of the recipes; and also Gillian Niblock of the Flour Advisory Bureau and Stella Dennis and Deborah Sack of Rank, Hovis McDougall, for technical advice and information.

Illustrated by Vanessa Luff
Edited by Sue Parish and Julia Bard
Designed by Clare Clements
Cover photography by James Jackson

Published by WI Books Limited,
39 Eccleston Street,
London SW1W 9NT

British Library Cataloguing in Publication Data
Mann, Lyn
The WI book of cakes.
1. Cake
I. Title
641.6'53 TX771
ISBN 0-900556-96-X

First impression 1985

Filmset by Text Filmsetters

Reproduced, printed and bound in Great Britain by
Hazell, Watson & Viney Limited,
Member of the BPCC Group,
Aylesbury, Bucks.

CONTENTS

INTRODUCTION

Cakes are not only satisfying and rewarding to make, they also provide welcome additions to family meal-times. Homemade cakes are wholesome, full of flavour and much cheaper than those you buy.

The different types of cakes are usually classified according to the proportion of fat to flour in the recipe and to the method of incorporating the fat. The exceptions are light sponges and Swiss rolls, made by whisking together eggs and sugar. These sponges are generally fat-free. The texture of cakes varies according to the method chosen. Plain cakes, made by rubbing the fat into the flour, have a more open and uneven texture, whereas rich cakes, made by creaming the fat with the sugar have a fine, even texture.

Rubbing-in method. This method, in which the fat is rubbed into the flour, is used for making cakes which have half or less than half fat to flour. These are known as plain cakes and include farmhouse cakes, rock cakes and scones (see chapter 1).

Creaming method. This method, in which the fat is creamed with the sugar, is used for cakes which have from half to equal quantities of fat to flour and to sugar. Cakes made by this method are known as rich cakes (see chapter 3) and include sandwich cakes, Madeira cakes and Christmas cakes.

Melting method. This is a very simple method whereby the fat is melted with the sugar before it is added to the other ingredients. Cakes made by this method include gingerbreads and some fruit cakes (see chapter 4).

Whisking method. In this method the eggs and sugar are whisked together to incorporate air and to give the traditional light, open texture (see chapter 2). Richer sponges have melted fat added.

All-in-one method. This is a very easy method of cake-making using soft-textured margarines. All the ingredients are beaten together for only 3-4 minutes. This method is generally used for rich cakes although it is possible to use it for plain cakes. The texture is more open than that produced by the more traditional methods (see chapter 4).

Equipment

Cakes can easily be made using a wooden spoon and a mixing bowl, but with so much labour-saving equipment available, time and energy can be saved. Electric mixers, with their beaters and whisks, are ideal for all types of cakes, but care should be taken to avoid over-beating as this could spoil the finished texture. Food processors are also useful, particularly for plain cakes made by the rubbing-in method and for the all-in-one method for rich cakes.

A wide variety of cake tins is available and it is best to build up a stock according to your requirements. Buy the best quality cake tins you can afford as they will last a long time. Non-stick tins can be useful, but they require careful treatment to avoid damaging the surface and are therefore not suitable for tray bakes, which are cut into shapes while the mixture is still in the tin.

A good basic cake-making set could include:

Two 18-cm (7-inch) straight-sided sandwich cake tins, about 4 cm (1½ inches) deep.

One 18-cm (7-inch) round cake tin about 9-10 cm (3½-4 inches) deep.

One 20-cm (8-inch) round cake tin about 9-10 cm (3½-4 inches) deep.

One 18-cm (7-inch) square cake tin about 9-10 cm (3½-4 inches) deep.

One 27 × 18-cm (10¾ × 7-inch) oblong tin about 4 cm (1½ inches) deep (good for gingerbreads, parkins etc.).

One 33 × 23 cm (13 × 9-inch) oblong tin about 1 cm (½ inch) deep (suitable for Swiss rolls, tray bakes etc.).

One set of bun tins.

One set of plain cutters and one set of fluted cutters.

Two cooling trays (the rack of a grill pan could easily double for a cooling tray).

One nylon sieve/strainer (for fine sieving of flour, raising agents, spices, icing sugar etc.).

Flours

Plain flour. This is the most versatile flour and is ideal for cake-making, either on its own or with the addition of a raising agent, according to the recipe. Strong plain flour is unsuitable for cakes.

Self-raising flour. This has a controlled, fixed proportion of raising agent added and is also suitable for plain cakes but would be unsuitable for some of the very rich, heavily-fruited cakes, where plain flour is preferable.

Special or 'S' self-raising flour. This is ideal for light-textured, sponge-type cakes as it can tolerate higher levels of sugar, fat and liquid and can produce larger cakes with an even, fine texture. It is a fine, soft, wheat flour, especially milled for sponge-making.

Wholemeal flour. On its own or mixed with white flour, this can be successfully used in farmhouse-type cakes and gingerbreads and, as well as giving a good, 'nutty' flavour, introduces extra fibre into the diet. Additional liquid added to the recipe ensures a good, moist cake.

Raising agents

Raising agents give lightness to the finished cake. They include baking powder (a blend of bicarbonate of soda and cream of tartar or other acid) and bicarbonate of soda, used either on its own in a strong-flavoured, dark cake mixture like gingerbread, or with a suitable acid ingredient like cream of tartar, sour milk, vinegar etc., as in scones. Air incorporated during cake-making is another raising agent.

Sugars

These vary in the size of grain and in colour. The coarser-grained sugars are suitable for plain cakes with their more open textures; the fine-grained sugars are better for rich cakes made by the creaming method.

The rich, dark, fine-grained sugars give flavour and colour to gingerbreads and special occasion cakes like Christmas cakes. Golden syrup and treacle, because they contain a sugar which does not crystallize, give a moist crumb to the finished cake and also add colour and flavour. However, syrups, treacle and also honey tend to make the cake liable to become too brown, so take care to follow the recipe, particularly when substituting these ingredients for some of the sugar.

Fruits and spices

Although fruits are now sold washed and ready for use, it is advisable to check thoroughly. If in doubt, wash and dry the fruit before use – particularly currants. Some raisins, especially if they are large, are better if lightly chopped before being used. Glacé cherries are preserved in a heavy syrup which causes them to sink in a cake mixture. It is advisable to halve or quarter cherries, wash and then dry thoroughly before use. Candied peel can be bought ready-chopped or in larger pieces according to choice. Spices add flavour and a beautiful aroma, but if packed ready-ground, buy only very small quantities, as they quickly become stale. Nutmeg is easy to buy as a whole spice and can be grated as required.

Fats and oils

Butter gives excellent flavour but is not quite so easy to cream as margarine. In most recipes either can be used.

The harder margarines which do not liquefy readily at room temperature are ideal for cake-making by the rubbing-in method, while the softer-textured and tub-packaged margarines, which tend to liquefy more readily, are better for the traditional creaming method and for the all-in-one method, where they are easily incorporated. Lard and dripping can also be used, but mainly in recipes where other ingredients add flavour.

Vegetable oils such as corn oil, sunflower oil, etc., can be used very successfully in cake-making. If substituting for solid fats in a recipe, a good guide is to use 2 tablespoonfuls oil to each 25 g (1 oz) solid fat. To compensate for some lack of aeration in the mixture, add 1 teaspoonful baking powder to each 100 g (4 oz) self-raising flour.

Preparation of tins

Careful preparation of baking tins is always advisable as the finished cake will then be uniform. For plain cakes, greasing the tins is often sufficient, but for richer cakes the tins should be greased and carefully lined with greaseproof paper. Cakes requiring long cooking usually benefit from being cooked in greased and lined tins. Light sponge cakes have a crisp finish if the tin is greased, then dusted lightly with a mixture of flour and caster sugar. Sandwich cake tins should be greased and only base-lined.

Baking

Oven temperatures given in recipes are just guidelines as two ovens rarely give the same results. Generally, the top third of the oven is the hottest, whilst the ideal position for cakes requiring long, slow cooking, is the middle of the oven. Cakes which cook quickly, like scones, should be placed as recommended in the recipes. Having positioned the shelves, set the oven about 15-20 minutes before you start cooking to allow time for pre-heating.

Try to avoid opening the oven door before at least half the recommended cooking time has elapsed as this could cause the cake to sink. It may be necessary to cover the cake to avoid over-browning, so carefully place a sheet of foil or a double thickness of greaseproof paper over the top of the tin.

Tests for whether the cake is cooked. The cake will be well risen, firm to the touch and beginning to shrink slightly from the sides of the tin.

Cooling

If you allow the cake to cool in the tin for the time suggested in the recipe, the cake will be firmer and easier to handle. When a cake has a light, fragile top, turn it out onto a cooling rack lined with a folded tea-towel; cover with a second cooling rack, then immediately invert both racks together and remove the top rack. This avoids marking the top of the cake – particularly important if entering a competition.

Microwave baking

Cakes baked in a microwave oven do not brown, but this can be overcome by using a frosting or icing, or by choosing recipes whose ingredients give the cake a naturally dark colour, e.g. chocolate, ginger or treacle.

Microwaved cakes will rise higher and are lighter than those conventionally baked. They are fragile, with a very tender crumb, but adding an extra egg, and reducing the liquid in the recipe by 2 tablespoonfuls will make the cake less fragile.

The best results are obtained from recipes which are rich in fat and eggs. Vegetable oil can be used very successfully in cakes baked in the microwave oven.

Follow the manufacturer's recommendations especially regarding suitable containers.

Storage

Rich cakes can be successfully stored if wrapped in greaseproof paper and kept in a cake tin or other suitable container. The richer the cake, the longer it will keep; plain cakes, because of their relatively low proportion of fat, are better eaten soon after baking as they tend to stale more quickly.

All cakes can be successfully frozen. If iced or decorated with frosting or butter cream, it is easier to freeze the cake uncovered, then wrap in a plastic bag when frozen.

Measurements

All the spoon measurements in this book are level unless stated otherwise.

Eggs are taken to be size 2 unless otherwise stated.

When following these recipes please use either the metric measurements or the imperial.

American equivalents

	Metric	Imperial	American
Butter, margarine	225g	8oz	1 cup
Flour	100g	4oz	1 cup
Currants	150g	5oz	1 cup
Sugar	200g	7oz	1 cup
Syrup	335g	11½oz	1 cup

An American pint is 16fl oz compared with the imperial pint of 20fl oz. A standard American cup measure is considered to hold 8fl oz.

DESIGN AND DECORATION

Design

A simple but neatly executed design can be most effective. It is advisable to avoid progressing to the more elaborate designs before you have mastered the more basic ones.

There are many excellent books available which give detailed instructions, but in general, the best results are achieved when you carefully consider the relation of the cake to the icing, the proportion and balance of the cake and avoid heavy decoration.

The texture of the cake should be complemented by the icing. Soft icings are suitable for light, textured cakes like sandwich cakes, layer cakes, sponges, etc. Royal icing and moulding icing are ideal for rich, heavily fruited cakes. Decoration should be considered in relation to the size of the cake, as too heavy a decoration looks unbalanced. When planning a tiered cake with the focal point in the centre of the top tier, the sides of the cake should be finished neatly but should not detract from the apex of the cake.

In a three-tiered cake, good proportion is important. Using cakes of 30 cm (12 inches), 20 cm (8 inches) and 10 cm (4 inches) diameter with a depth of 7.5 cm (3 inches) gives a good result.

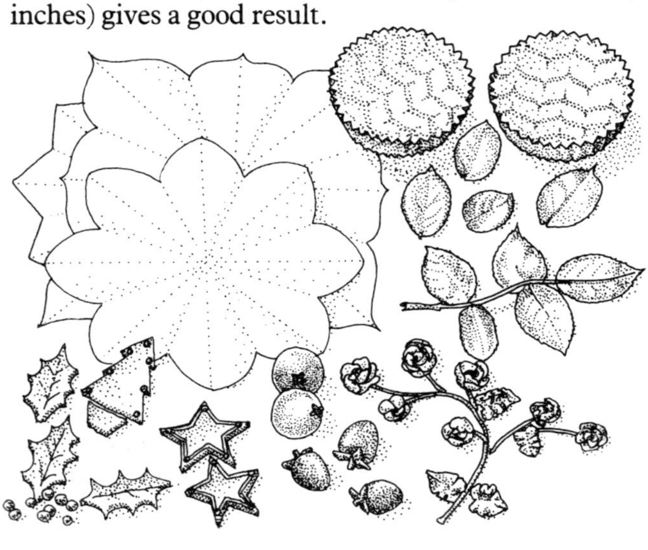

Equipment

You can achieve good results with fairly simple equipment. A palette knife or a plastic icing comb can produce a simple design, whilst for piping soft icings, a metal or nylon No.6 star nozzle is ideal. For Royal icing, a No.1 or No.2 plain nozzle and a No.6 or No.8 star nozzle can be used to produce a variety of patterns.

Nylon piping bags can be bought, but it is quite simple to make your own using good quality greaseproof paper. These are cheap and ideal for piping small quantities of icing.

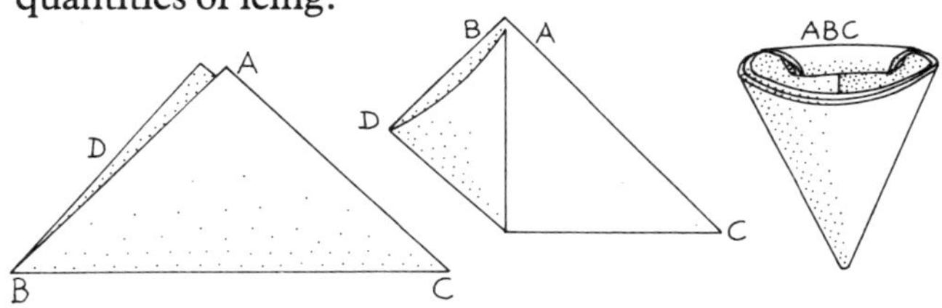

1. Cut a 25 cm (10-inch) square of greaseproof paper and fold in half to form a triangle.
2. Fold point B to meet point A and hold in place.
3. Roll point C over towards point D and bring it behind point D. Pull point C into place to meet point AB at the top. Holding these three points together, make a double fold inwards and crease well to secure.

It is a good idea to make a supply of these greaseproof paper bags, then if one bursts, it is easy to slide it inside a new bag and continue piping.

To prepare the greaseproof paper bag for use, cut a very small piece from the tip, fit in the piping tube so not more than half the tube protrudes at the bottom of the bag. If necessary, re-cut to allow the tube to fit. If the tube protrudes too much, undue pressure is put on the paper and the bag tends to burst.

Using a palette knife or icing comb. An effective decoration can be made on a square or oblong cake by drawing a palette knife across the surface of the soft icing, working from one side to the other. On a round cake, draw the knife from the centre to the edge of the cake, making a series of shallow curves radiating out. An icing comb can be used to make a straight, ridged finish or, by moving the comb slightly from side to side, a wavy finish. A fork can also be used to make a similar design.

Feather icing. This is a simple, but most effective way of using contrasting colours of glacé icing to create different designs. Make up the required amount of glacé icing according to the size of the cake. Place 3 teaspoonfuls of icing in a small basin and add sufficient food colouring to give a deep colour. If the base coat icing is to be white or any other pale colour, it is important to make the contrast a very deep colour otherwise the effect will be disappointing.

Using a greaseproof paper piping bag (see page 11) without a piping tube (and therefore without the tip of the bag being removed), place the contrasting colour icing in the bag and fold over the top of the paper to secure it. Using a palette knife, spread the base coat icing over the cake to just within about 5 mm (¼ inch) of the edge; the weight of the icing will allow it to flow to the edge. Cut just the tip off the greaseproof icing paper bag and quickly pipe parallel lines, about 2.5 cm (1 inch) apart across the cake.

Using either a skewer or the point of a knife, quickly draw it through just the surface of the icing, at right angles to the piped lines and about 2.5 cm (1 inch) apart. Turn the cake around and repeat, drawing the skewer or knife between the first lines but in the opposite direction. Allow to set before moving the cake.

It is important to work quickly when using this technique as glacé icing sets quickly. Once the base coat has been applied, pipe the contrast colour at once.

As a variation, pipe a continuous spiral of contrasting coloured icing, beginning at the centre of the cake. Draw the skewer or knife from the centre to the edge, making a "spider's web" effect. By drawing the skewer or knife from the edge to the centre, a petalled or flower effect can be created.

Piping

The consistency of the icing is most important in

creating an effective decoration. Soft icings usually require the addition of a little sieved icing sugar to ensure a design which will hold its shape. A good guide to the correct consistency is to mix the icing until it will just hold a soft peak when the spoon is lifted out.

The consistency required for piping Royal icing varies according to the chosen design. Small plain nozzles used mainly for writing, piping lines and dots etc., require a soft peak consistency, whilst the star nozzles used for piping rosettes, stars, shells, etc. require a stiff peak consistency, otherwise the pattern will tend to lose its sharp outline.

Simple decorations for Christmas cakes

Using almond paste. Holly leaves, holly berries, and small crackers can all be made cheaply and successfully with any left-over almond paste (see page 81), coloured by food colouring.

Holly leaves and berries. Mix in sufficient green colouring to give a good depth of colour. Roll out the almond paste thinly on a working surface very lightly dusted with cornflour. Cut into strips about 1.5 cm (¾ inch) wide, then cut into diamond shapes. Using the base of a small icing nozzle as a cutter, shape the diamond into a holly leaf shape. Lightly mark in the veins of the leaf and allow it to dry out. The holly leaves will dry into an attractive curved shape if they are placed over the back of an upturned spoon or a rolling pin. Use red colouring mixed into almond paste to make various-sized holly berries, and allow to dry out.

Crackers. Colour almond paste into a variety of different colours. Using a small amount, roll out under the palms of your hands, to a long thin roll about the size of a cigarette, or larger if desired. Cut into lengths of about 2.5-4 cm (1-1½ inches).

Using the back of a knife, make a small indent a little way in from each end of the roll for the shoulders of the cracker. Hollow out each end of the roll using a cocktail stick or small skewer. Allow to dry out. Decorate by piping Royal icing into stars, initials etc., and by outlining each end in Royal icing.

Sugar bells. These are most attractive, not only as

decorations for Christmas cakes, but for other special occasion cakes like silver or golden weddings. They are cheap to make but you will need to buy small, bell-shaped moulds without the central clapper or striker.

Mix about 50g (2oz) granulated sugar with just enough raw egg white to give a consistency in which the sugar is just beginning to hold together (like the consistency of sand for making sand castles). Pack the sugar into the moulds and press in firmly. Invert the mould, give it a sharp shake and the sugar bell will fall out. If the sugar is too wet, it will stick to the mould; if it is too dry, it will crumble. Either can easily be rectified by adding more sugar or more egg white.

Make more than you need to allow for any breakages when finishing the bells. Turn the bells out onto a sheet of foil placed over a board or plate, and dry out at room temperature for about 2 hours.

After drying out, the bells will be firm on the outside but the centres will still be soft. Using the point of a small knife, carefully remove the soft sugar, leaving a firm, hollow bell. The soft sugar which is removed can be used to make further bells or spread out and allowed to dry. It makes an attractive, glistening finish to sprinkle over cakes.

When the bells are thoroughly dry, pipe a small line of Royal icing inside to simulate the clapper or striker and place a small silver cachou at the end of the clapper.

Colouring may be added to the mixture. A very pretty effect can be achieved using yellow, red or green food colouring combined with white to give a frosting. In this case, pack the bell mould to just within its edge with coloured sugar, then fill to the brim with white sugar mixture. When hollowed out after drying, the bells will have a frosted edge.

Chocolate work

Interesting shapes in chocolate make most effective decorations. Plain chocolate is better than milk chocolate as it sets harder. Couverture and cooking chocolate are ideal and set fairly quickly, but you must allow additional time if using a richer plain chocolate as this takes considerably longer to set.

It is advisable to grate the chocolate coarsely as it will melt more quickly and not overheat.

To melt the chocolate. Place in a small basin and suspend over a pan of gently steaming water, making sure the bottom of the basin is not touching the water. Heat gently, stirring occasionally, and take care that no water gets mixed into the melting chocolate as this could spoil the texture.

Chocolate rose leaves. Use fresh, mature rose leaves in good condition. Wash lightly and dry thoroughly. Using a small paint brush, brush melted chocolate over the underside of each leaf, making sure the entire surface is covered. Place the leaves, chocolate side uppermost, on a piece of foil and allow to become quite hard and set. Carefully peel off the rose leaf, leaving the chocolate leaf. These may be stored in layers of tissue or kitchen paper until required.

Chocolate shapes. Cover a small board with a sheet of foil and spread the melted chocolate in an even layer over the foil. Lift the corners of the foil and allow the foil to drop back in place as this levels the chocolate. Allow to reach almost setting point (the chocolate will begin to lose its gloss) then mark into shapes.

Squares. Using a ruler as a guide, cut chocolate into the required size.

Rounds or crescents. Use a small plain cutter to cut rounds; remove part of the round to form a crescent.

Triangles. Cut squares in half.

To remove the cut shapes, allow the chocolate to set hard, then carefully peel away the foil.

FAMILY CAKES

These economical recipes are for both large and small cakes and include recipes for tray bakes and scones. They are made by the rubbing-in method and are best eaten freshly baked.

CHOCOLATE WALNUT CAKE

350 g (12 oz) self-raising flour
½ tsp ground cinnamon
½ tsp mixed spice
175 g (6 oz) margarine
50 g (2 oz) chocolate
50 g (2 oz) walnuts
175 g (6 oz) raisins
175 g (6 oz) demerara sugar
2 eggs
about 150 ml (¼ pint) milk
1 tbsp demerara sugar for topping

Heat the oven to 180°C (350°F) mark 4. Lightly grease a 20-cm (8-inch) round or an 18-cm (7-inch) square cake tin and line with greaseproof paper. Lightly grease the lining paper.

Sieve the flour with the spices into a mixing bowl and rub in the margarine. Roughly chop the chocolate and walnuts. Wash and dry the raisins. Stir the nuts, chocolate and raisins into the rubbed-in mixture together with the sugar. Lightly beat the eggs and stir into the dry ingredients together with three-quarters of the milk. Mix thoroughly, adding sufficient of the remaining milk to give a soft dropping consistency. Place in the prepared tin, smooth over the top and sprinkle with the sugar for topping.

Bake for 1 hour then reduce the oven temperature to 150°C (300°F) mark 2 and cook for a further 30-60 minutes or until the cake is firm to the touch and has begun to shrink from the sides of the tin. Cool the cake in the tin for 10-15 minutes, then turn out onto a cooling rack.

FARMHOUSE CIDER CAKE

275 g (10 oz) mixed dried fruit
350 g (12 oz) self-raising flour
pinch of salt
175 g (6 oz) margarine
175 g (6 oz) demerara sugar
zest of 1 orange
2 eggs
2 tbsp orange marmalade
scant 150 ml (¼ pint) cider

Heat the oven to 180°C (350°F) mark 4. Lightly grease a 20-cm (8-inch) round or 18-cm (7-inch) square cake tin, line with greaseproof paper and grease the paper.

Wash and dry the mixed dried fruits. Sieve the flour and salt into a mixing bowl and rub in the margarine until the mixture resembles fine breadcrumbs. Stir in the sugar, prepared dried fruits and orange zest, mixing thoroughly. Beat the eggs lightly and stir into the dry mixture, together with the marmalade and most of the cider. Mix well to a moderately stiff consistency, adding more cider as necessary. Place in the prepared cake tin, smooth over the top and hollow out the centre a little.

Bake for 1 hour, then reduce the oven temperature to 150°C (300°F) mark 2, cover with foil or a sheet of greaseproof paper, and bake for a further 45-60 minutes or until the cake has begun to shrink from the sides of the tin and is firm to the touch. Cool in the tin for about 30 minutes then turn out onto a cooling rack.

HONEY CAKE

100 g (4 oz) currants
100 g (4 oz) sultanas
50 g (2 oz) glacé cherries
175 g (6 oz) self-raising flour
100 g (4 oz) margarine
100 g (4 oz) soft brown sugar
50 g (2 oz) ground almonds
3 eggs
1 tbsp honey
1 tbsp black treacle

Heat the oven to 180°C (350°F) mark 4. Lightly grease and line an 18-cm (7-inch) round cake tin; lightly grease the lining paper.

Wash and dry the currants, sultanas and cherries; quarter the cherries.

Sieve the flour into a mixing bowl and rub in the margarine. Stir in the sugar, ground almonds and prepared fruit. Lightly beat the eggs. Make a well in the dry mixture and add the honey, treacle and the eggs. Mix thoroughly, then place in the prepared tin, hollowing out the centre just a little.

Bake for 40 minutes, then reduce the oven temperature to 170°C (325°F) mark 3, and continue cooking for a further 40-45 minutes until the cake has begun to shrink slightly from the sides of the tin and is firm to the touch.

Cool in the tin for 15 minutes then turn out onto a cooling rack.

DELIGHTFUL CRUNCH

225 g (8 oz) plain flour
2 tbsp icing sugar
100 g (4 oz) margarine

Topping
2 eggs
175 g (6 oz) caster sugar
75 g (3 oz) glacé cherries
75 g (3 oz) chopped walnuts
75 g (3 oz) desiccated coconut

Heat the oven to 150°C (300°F) mark 2. Lightly grease a large Swiss roll tin measuring 33 × 25 cm (13 × 10 inches).

Sieve the flour and icing sugar, then rub in the margarine until the mixture resembles fine breadcrumbs. Press the mixture evenly but firmly into the prepared tin.

To make the topping, lightly whisk the eggs and beat with the sugar until very thick and creamy in consistency. Chop the cherries roughly and fold into the egg mixture, together with the nuts and coconut. Spread evenly over the pastry.

Bake for about 40 minutes or until golden brown and firm to the touch.

Allow to cool in the tin for 30 minutes then cut into fingers before the mixture is cold.

CHERRY AND PINEAPPLE CAKES

Makes 12

100 g (4 oz) plain flour
pinch of salt
50 g (2 oz) ground rice
1 tsp baking powder
65 g (2½ oz) margarine
65 g (2½ oz) granulated sugar
25 g (1 oz) glacé pineapple
25 g (1 oz) glacé cherries
1 egg
milk to mix
a little caster sugar

Heat the oven to 200°C (400°F) mark 6. Lightly grease a baking tray. Sieve the flour with the salt, ground rice and baking powder, then rub in the margarine. Mix in the sugar and roughly chopped glacé fruits.

Lightly beat the egg and mix it into the dry ingredients. The consistency should be stiff, but a little milk may be required to bind the ingredients together.

Using two teaspoons, shape the mixture into 12 rough mounds on the baking tray, leaving space between each mound. Sprinkle with a little caster sugar and bake for 12-15 minutes until firm to the touch and golden in colour. Place on a cooling rack.

FARMHOUSE FRUIT CAKE

175-225 g (6-8 oz) mixed dried fruits
225 g (8 oz) self-raising flour
pinch of salt
1 tsp mixed spice
½ tsp ground nutmeg
100 g (4 oz) margarine
100 g (4 oz) granulated or demerara sugar
25 g (1 oz) chopped peel
1 egg
1 tbsp marmalade or golden syrup
150 ml (¼ pint) milk

Heat the oven to 180°C (350°F) mark 4. Lightly grease and flour a 15-cm (6-inch) round cake tin, or a loaf tin measuring 21 × 12 cm (8½ × 4½ inches). Wash and dry the mixed dried fruits.

Sieve the flour, salt and spices together and rub in the margarine. Stir in the sugar, prepared dried fruits and chopped peel. Whisk the egg lightly and add to the dry ingredients together with the marmalade or golden syrup. Add sufficient milk to give a soft dropping consistency.

Place in the prepared tin and smooth over the top, hollowing out the middle a little. Bake for about 1 hour, then reduce the oven temperature to 150°C (300°F) mark 2, and bake for up to 30 minutes or until the cake has begun to shrink from the sides of the tin and is firm to the touch.

CHERRY AND FRUIT FINGERS

175 g (6 oz) plain flour
1 tbsp icing sugar
½ tsp salt
75 g (3 oz) margarine and lard, mixed
1½ tbsp water
5 tbsp lemon curd

Topping
100 g (4 oz) margarine
100 g (4 oz) caster sugar
2 eggs
100 g (4 oz) self-raising flour
50 g (2 oz) glacé cherries
10 g (2 oz) currants

Heat the oven to 200°C (400°F) mark 6. Sieve the flour, icing sugar and salt into a mixing bowl; rub in the mixed fat until the mixture resembles fine breadcrumbs. Bind together with the water to form a firm, but not crumbly, pastry. Knead lightly to remove any cracks. Roll out to a thickness of about 5 mm (¼ inch) and use to line a 30 × 20-cm (12 × 8-inch) Swiss roll tin. Trim the edges and spread with the lemon curd.

For the topping, cream the margarine and sugar together until light and fluffy. Lightly beat the eggs and beat into the creamed mixture. Sieve the flour and carefully fold into the egg/fat mixture. Chop the glacé cherries coarsely and add with the currants.

Spread this mixture over the lemon curd.

Bake for 10 minutes then reduce the oven temperature to 180°C (350°F) mark 4, and bake for a further 20-25 minutes or until the mixture begins to shrink from the sides of the tin and is firm to the touch.

Cool in the tin for 15-20 minutes, then cut into fingers or squares.

AFTER CHRISTMAS CAKES

Makes 10-12

225 g (8 oz) self-raising flour
pinch of salt
100 g (4 oz) margarine
75 g (3 oz) granulated sugar
50 g (2 oz) plain or milk chocolate, fairly finely chopped
25 g (1 oz) Brazil nuts, chopped
1 egg
1 tbsp milk
½ tsp vanilla flavouring

Heat the oven to 200°C (400°F) mark 6. Lightly grease a baking tray. Sieve the flour and salt; rub in the margarine until the mixture resembles fine breadcrumbs. Stir in the sugar, chocolate and Brazil nuts. Beat the egg lightly; combine with almost all the milk and add the vanilla flavouring. Mix thoroughly with the dry ingredients to form a very stiff mixture which will just bind together. Add the extra milk if necessary.

Shape into 10-12 rough mounds on the prepared baking tray. Bake for about 12-15 minutes or until firm to the touch. Place on a cooling rack.

These cakes are great favourites and are a good way of using up any nuts and chocolate remaining after Christmas.

VIENNA SLICES

100 g (4 oz) self-raising flour
pinch of salt
25 g (1 oz) margarine
25 g (1 oz) lard
about 4 tsp water

Filling
100 g (4 oz) finely crumbled cake crumbs
25 g (1 oz) ground almonds
25 g (1 oz) melted butter
1 tbsp apricot jam

Topping
3 egg whites
150 g (5 oz) caster sugar
25 g (1 oz) granulated sugar

Heat the oven to 200°C (400°F) mark 6. Sieve the flour with the salt and rub in the fats. Bind the mixture together with enough water to make a firm but not crumbly pastry. Knead the pastry lightly to remove any cracks, then roll out to a 25-cm (10-inch) square, 5 mm (¼ inch) thick. Use to line a shallow tin about 20 cm (8 inches) square. Trim the edges.

To make the filling, mix the cake crumbs with the ground almonds, then stir in the melted butter and the apricot jam. Mix thoroughly and spread evenly in the pastry-lined tin. Bake for 18-20 minutes. Allow to cool in the tin. Reduce the oven temperature to 150°C (300°F) mark 2.

To make the topping, whisk the egg whites until they form stiff peaks, then lightly fold in the sugars. Spread the meringue evenly over the cooked mixture. Bake for a further 30 minutes. Cool in the tin, then cut into slices.

CHERRY AND LEMON COOKIES

Makes 18

225 g (8 oz) self-raising flour
100 g (4 oz) margarine
100 g (4 oz) granulated sugar
50 g (2 oz) glacé cherries
finely grated zest of ½ lemon
1 egg
1 tbsp milk
2 tsp lemon juice

Topping
50 g (2 oz) icing sugar
25 g (1 oz) granulated sugar
2 tsp lemon juice

Heat the oven to 200°C (400°F) mark 6. Lightly grease two baking trays. Sieve the flour and rub in the margarine until the mixture resembles fine breadcrumbs. Stir in the sugar. Chop the cherries roughly and mix in, together with the lemon zest. Mix thoroughly. Beat the egg lightly with the milk and lemon juice. Add to the dry ingredients and use a fork to mix to a stiff dough.

Using two teaspoons, shape into about 18 rough mounds on the greased trays, allowing room for the cookies to spread a little. Bake for 12-15 minutes until firm to the touch and golden brown in colour. Place on a cooling rack.

To make the topping, mix the icing and granulated sugars with sufficient lemon juice to form a thick coating consistency. Spoon over the top of the warm cookies.

YORKSHIRE TEA BUNS

Makes 18-20

450 g (1 lb) plain flour
pinch of salt
2 tsp baking powder
100 g (4 oz) margarine
100 g (4 oz) granulated sugar
1 egg
about 275 ml (½ pint) milk
a little milk and sugar to glaze

Heat the oven to 220°C (425°F) mark 7. Lightly grease two baking trays. Sieve the flour, salt and baking powder. Rub in the margarine. Stir in the sugar. Lightly beat the egg and add to the dry ingredients together with enough milk to form a soft, but not sticky, dough.

Knead very lightly to remove any cracks, then roll out to a thickness of 1 cm (½ inch). Cut into 5-cm (2-inch) squares and fold over to make triangles. Place on prepared baking trays, brush with milk and sprinkle with a little sugar.

Bake for 12-15 minutes. Place on a cooling rack. To serve, split open and butter.

COCONUT AND CHOCOLATE CRUNCH

170 g (6 oz) self-raising flour
pinch of salt
3 heaped tsp cocoa
150 g (5 oz) margarine
75 g (3 oz) sugar
100 g (4 oz) desiccated coconut

Topping
50 g (2 oz) cooking chocolate

Heat the oven to 140°C (275°F) mark 1. Lightly grease a Swiss roll tin measuring 30 × 20 cm (12 × 8 inches).

Sieve the flour, salt and cocoa into a mixing bowl. Rub in the margarine until the mixture resembles fine breadcrumbs. Stir in the sugar and desiccated coconut. Knead thoroughly, then press the mixture, firmly and evenly, into the prepared tin.

Bake for 25-30 minutes. Allow to cool in the tin. To make the topping, grate the chocolate coarsely and place in a small bowl, or on a heat-resistant plate. Suspend the chocolate over a pan of gently steaming water until it is melted and smooth in consistency. Spread evenly over the cooled coconut base. When almost set, cut into fingers or squares.

LEMON SOURS

75 g (3 oz) margarine
75 g (3 oz) plain flour

Filling
2 eggs
150 g (5 oz) soft brown sugar
75 g (3 oz) desiccated coconut
75 g (3 oz) chopped nuts
1/2 tsp vanilla flavouring
1/8 tsp baking powder

Icing
4 tbsp icing sugar
1 tbsp lemon juice
1 tsp lemon zest

Heat the oven to 190°C (375°F) mark 5. Cut the margarine into the flour until the mixture resembles breadcrumbs, then press firmly and evenly into a 20-cm (8-inch) shallow, square baking tin. Bake for 10 minutes.

To make the filling, beat the eggs slightly and stir in the sugar, coconut, nuts, vanilla flavouring and baking powder. Spread this over the baked mixture, working well into the corners. Bake for 20 minutes at the same temperature.

To make the icing, sieve the icing sugar, then mix into the lemon juice and zest to form a creamy frosting. Spread this over the baked mixture as soon as it is removed from the oven. Cool in the tin, then cut into squares.

WELSH CAKES

175 g (6 oz) margarine
50 g (2 oz) lard
100 g (4 oz) currants
450 g (1 lb) self-raising flour
pinch of salt
¼ tsp mixed spice
¼ tsp ground nutmeg
200 g (7 oz) caster sugar
2 eggs
a little milk to mix

Blend the margarine and lard together. Wash and dry the currants. Sieve the flour, salt and spices into a mixing bowl, then rub in the fats. Stir in the sugar and currants. Lightly beat the eggs and mix into the dry ingredients, adding enough milk to mix to a firm dough.

Knead lightly, on a floured surface, then roll out to a thickness of 1 cm (½ inch). Cut into rounds, using a floured 5-cm (2-inch) fluted cutter. Cook on both sides, to a golden brown, on a moderately hot preheated girdle or in a strong, heavy-based frying pan.

DATE SLICES

225 g (8 oz) stoned dates
juice of 1 orange, plus enough water to make up to 275 ml (½ pint)
finely grated zest of 1 orange
100 g (4 oz) self-raising flour
1 tsp bicarbonate of soda
100 g (4 oz) rolled oats
175 g (6 oz) caster sugar
100 g (4 oz) margarine

Heat the oven to 180°C (350°F) mark 4. Lightly grease a 30 × 23-cm (12 × 9-inch) Swiss roll tin.

Chop the dates roughly and place in a saucepan with the water and orange juice. Bring to the boil and cook until just soft; stir in the orange zest. Allow to cool a little.

Sieve the flour and bicarbonate of soda thoroughly. Stir in the rolled oats and sugar, then rub in the margarine. Press half this mixture into the prepared tin in a firm, even layer. Spread the date mixture over the top and cover with the remaining oat mixture, pressing lightly to make firm.

Bake for 20-30 minutes until golden in colour. Mark into bars or fingers and allow to cool in the tin.

BASIC SCONES

225 g (8 oz) self-raising flour
pinch of salt
25 g (1 oz) granulated sugar (optional)

Or
225 g (8 oz) plain flour
3 tsp baking powder
pinch of salt
25 g (1 oz) granulated sugar (optional)

Or
225 g (8 oz) plain flour
1 tsp bicarbonate of soda
2 tsp cream of tartar
pinch of salt
25 g (1 oz) granulated sugar (optional)

Plus
40 g (1½ oz) margarine
150 ml (¼ pint) milk or milk and water mixed

Heat the oven to 230°C (450°F) mark 8. Lightly grease a baking tray. Sieve the flour, very carefully, with the raising agents and salt to ensure even distribution. Rub in the margarine until the mixture resembles fine breadcrumbs. Add the sugar, if used. Quickly bind together, with the milk or milk and water mixture, to a soft, but not sticky dough.

Knead lightly until smooth and free of cracks. Roll out the dough, using an even pressure, on a floured working surface, to a thickness of 1 cm (½ inch). Cut into rounds, using a floured, 2-inch cutter (avoid twisting the cutter, as this results in an oval-shaped scone). Carefully transfer the scones to the prepared baking tray. Brush the tops with milk or dredge lightly with flour.

Bake for 7-10 minutes. Place on a cooling rack.

Alternative shaping
Shape the scone dough into a round, approximately 20 cm (8 inches) in diameter. Place on the prepared baking tray; cut half-way through the dough dividing it into eight wedges, and brush with milk. Bake for 20-25 minutes until golden brown and firm to the touch.

Variations
(1) Sultana: add 50 g (2 oz) sultanas and 25 g (1 oz) granulated sugar to the dry ingredients.
(2) Honey: substitute 1 tablespoonful honey for 1 tablespoonful milk.
(3) Cherry and orange: add the zest of 1 orange and 50 g (2 oz) finely chopped, washed and dried glacé cherries to the dry ingredients.

(4) Wholemeal: substitute 100 g (4 oz) wholemeal flour for 100 g (4 oz) white flour – this may require more liquid to mix as wholemeal flour is more absorbent.
(5) Yoghurt: substitute 4 tablespoonfuls natural yoghurt for 4 tablespoonfuls milk.
(6) Treacle: add 1-2 tablespoonfuls treacle or syrup with the milk, sieve ½ teaspoonful ground ginger and ½ teaspoonful mixed spice with the flour.
(7) Cheese: add ½ teaspoonful mustard powder and a good pinch of cayenne pepper to the flour; stir in 75-100 g (3-4 oz) finely grated strong-flavoured cheese.
(8) Herbs: add 1 teaspoonful mustard powder to the flour and stir in 1 tablespoonful finely chopped, mixed fresh herbs (e.g. parsley, chives, sage, marjoram).

APPLE SCONES

225 g (8 oz) self-raising flour
1 tsp baking powder
pinch of salt
50 g (2 oz) margarine
50 g (2 oz) granulated sugar
1 medium-sized cooking apple, peeled, cored and chopped
scant 150 ml (¼ pint) milk

Glaze
a little milk
25 g (1 oz) demerara sugar

Heat the oven to 200°C (400°F) mark 6. Lightly grease a baking tray. Sieve the flour, baking powder and salt into a mixing bowl. Rub in the margarine until the mixture resembles fine breadcrumbs. Stir in the sugar. Stir the apple into the mixture. Mix together, using a fork, with sufficient milk to give a soft, but not sticky, dough.

Knead lightly on a floured surface then roll out to a circle, about 20 cm (8 inches) in diameter. Place on a lightly greased baking tray and mark into eight wedges. Brush the top with milk and sprinkle with demerara sugar.

Bake for 20-25 minutes until well risen, golden and firm to the touch. Place on a cooling rack.

SPONGES, GÂTEAUX AND SWISS ROLLS

This chapter contains recipes for delicious light sponges made by the whisking method. Some are enriched by adding melted butter so they will keep fresh for a longer time. Sponges form the base for many exciting iced gâteaux as well as being convenient to have in the freezer to use as the base of fruit and cream desserts.

SPONGE CAKE (1)

3 eggs
75 g (3 oz) caster sugar
75 g (3 oz) plain flour
1 tbsp hot water
finely grated zest of 1 lemon or a few drops of vanilla flavouring
whipped double cream or jam for filling
icing sugar to dust

Heat the oven to 180°C (350°F) mark 4. Lightly grease and line the base of an 18-cm (7-inch) round cake tin and grease the lining paper. Dust the tin with a mixture of flour and caster sugar, shaking out any surplus (this gives the sponge a crisp, sugary crust).

Place the eggs and the caster sugar in a roomy mixing bowl. Whisk until just blended, then place over a pan of gently steaming water and whisk until doubled in bulk and the whisk leaves a distinct trail when lifted out. Remove from the hot water and continue whisking until the mixture is cool and the consistency of lightly whipped cream. Sieve the flour, a tablespoonful at a time, into the bowl and fold in lightly using the side of a metal spoon. Fold in the hot water and the chosen flavouring.

Place in the prepared tin and bake for about 25-30 minutes or until golden in colour, firm to the touch and beginning to shrink from the sides of the tin. Allow to cool in the tin for 3-4 minutes then turn out onto a cooling rack.

This cake may be filled with whipped cream and jam and served lightly dusted with sieved icing sugar.

Variation
This sponge may be halved, filled with flavoured butter cream, fresh fruit and cream or used as the base for a gâteau instead of a Genoese sponge.

SPONGE CAKE (2)

3 eggs
75 g (3 oz) caster sugar
75 g (3 oz) plain flour
1 tbsp hot water
finely grated zest of 1 lemon or a few drops of vanilla flavouring

Heat the oven to 180°C (350°F) mark 4. Lightly grease and line the base of an 18-cm (7-inch) round cake tin and grease the lining paper. Dust the tin with a mixture of flour and caster sugar to give the sponge a crispy, sugary crust.

Separate the eggs and place the egg whites in a roomy mixing bowl. Whisk the egg whites until they form stiff peaks. Whisk in 25 g (1 oz) of the sugar together with one egg yolk, repeating this with the remaining egg yolks and sugar. Lightly fold in the sieved flour together with the hot water and chosen flavouring.

Place in the prepared tin and bake for about 25-30 minutes until golden in colour, firm to the touch and beginning to shrink slightly from the sides of the tin.

Allow to cool in the tin for 3-4 minutes then turn out on to a cooling rack. Finish as desired.

SPONGE DROPS

75 g (3 oz) plain flour
2 tbsp cornflour
2 eggs
75 g (3 oz) caster sugar
extra caster sugar to dredge

Heat the oven to 190°C (375°F) mark 5. Line two baking sheets with greaseproof paper cut to the exact size of the baking sheets. Do not grease the paper or the baking sheets.

Sieve the flour with the cornflour. Place the eggs and caster sugar in a roomy mixing bowl, whisk together to blend, then place over a pan of gently steaming water, making sure the base of the bowl is not sitting in the water, and whisk until the mixture begins to hold a trail. The mixture should be thick and creamy. Remove the mixing bowl from the water and continue to whisk the mixture until it has cooled and has the consistency of lightly whipped cream.

Sieve the flour mixture into the bowl and, using either a spatula or the edge of a metal spoon, fold in very lightly until blended.

Place the mixture in a forcing bag fitted with a 1-cm (½-inch) plain nozzle and pipe onto the prepared baking sheets into rounds about 4-cm (1½-inch) in diameter. Dredge lightly with caster sugar and bake for about 10-12 minutes or until pale golden in colour and firm to the touch.

Allow to cool on the baking trays for 5 minutes then slide a palette knife under each sponge drop and lift onto a cooling rack.

Sponge drops may be served as an accompaniment to cream desserts, ice creams or sandwiched together with whipped cream, fresh strawberries, etc.

CHOCOLATE-FILLED GENOESE CAKE

4 egg whites
100 g (4 oz) caster sugar
6 egg yolks
75 g (3 oz) plain flour
50 g (2 oz) melted butter

Filling
225 g (8 oz) plain chocolate
75 g (3 oz) caster sugar
275 ml (½ pint) double or whipping cream

Heat the oven to 180°C (350°F) mark 4. Grease and base-line two 20-cm (8-inch) sandwich tins and lightly grease the lining paper.

Place the egg whites in a large mixing bowl and whisk until they will stand in stiff peaks. Fold in the sugar, a tablespoonful at a time, adding one egg yolk each time. Finally fold in the remaining egg yolks. Sieve the flour and fold in, very lightly, adding the melted butter around the inside edge of the bowl with the last addition of flour. Place in the prepared tins and bake for about 25-30 minutes or until golden in colour, firm to the touch and beginning to shrink from the sides of the tin.

Allow to cool in the tin for 4-5 minutes then turn out onto a cooling rack.

For the filling, grate the chocolate and place in a heavy-based saucepan with the sugar and cream. Cook over a gentle heat until the sugar and chocolate are dissolved. Place in a basin and allow to cool, stirring occasionally to give a smooth texture.

Cut each sandwich sponge in half and spread with the chocolate filling to make a four-layer cake. Use the remaining chocolate filling to coat the top and sides of the cake. Decorate if desired.

GENOESE SPONGE CAKE

75 g (3 oz) plain flour
pinch of salt
3 eggs
75 g (3 oz) caster sugar
50 g (2 oz) unsalted butter, melted

Heat the oven to 180°C (350°F) mark 4. Lightly grease and line the base of an 18-cm (7-inch) round cake tin and lightly grease the lining paper. Sieve the flour and salt.

Place the eggs and sugar in a roomy mixing bowl, whisk together to blend, then place the bowl over a pan of gently steaming water, making sure the base of the bowl is above the surface of the water.

Whisk steadily until the mixture thickens, doubles in bulk and leaves a well-defined trail on the surface. Remove from the heat and continue whisking until the mixture is cool and has thickened to the consistency of lightly whipped cream.

Sieve the flour, a tablespoonful at a time, into the bowl and fold in very lightly. Pour in the melted butter around the inside edge of the bowl and fold in very quickly and evenly.

Place in the prepared tin and bake for 20-30 minutes or until golden in colour, firm to the touch and beginning to shrink slightly from the sides of the tin. Allow to cool for 3-4 minutes then turn out onto a cooling rack.

When cold, fill and decorate as desired.

Variations

(1) Chocolate: substitute 15 g (½ oz) cocoa for 15 g (½ oz) flour and add a few drops of vanilla flavouring.

(2) Coffee: add 2 teaspoonfuls coffee essence with the egg and sugar mixture.

(3) Lemon or orange: add the finely grated zest of 1 lemon or orange to the whisked mixture.

ICED FANCY CAKES

1 recipe quantity Genoese sponge mixture (see page 32) or 1 recipe quantity creamed mixture (see page 48)

flavouring as desired (see variations below and overleaf)

Heat the oven to 190°C (375°F) mark 5. Line a 28 × 18-cm (11 × 7-inch) Swiss roll tin and lightly grease the lining paper.

Place the mixture in the prepared tin and smooth well into the corners. Bake for about 15 minutes or until firm to the touch and beginning to shrink from the sides of the tin.

Allow to cool for 4-5 minutes then turn out onto a cooling rack and remove the lining paper. When cold, this sponge is ideal for cutting into various shapes for icing and decorating.

Variations

(1) Mocha sponge fancy: using a small, circular cutter about 2.5-4 cm (1-1½ inches) in diameter, cut out the required number of sponge bases.

Decorate (as follows) with a small amount of coffee-flavoured glacé icing (see page 86), a small amount of coffee-flavoured butter cream (see page 90) and chopped walnuts.

Coat the sides of the sponge with warmed apricot glaze, if using (see page 93). Allow to set.

Spread the sides with coffee butter cream and coat with finely chopped walnuts. Pipe a small border of butter cream around the top edge of each sponge and run the coffee glacé icing into the centre. Allow to set.

(2) Glacé iced almond fancy: cut out the required number of triangular or diamond shapes from the cold sponge, each side measuring about 4 cm (1½ inches). Brush with warmed apricot glaze (see page 93) and allow to set.

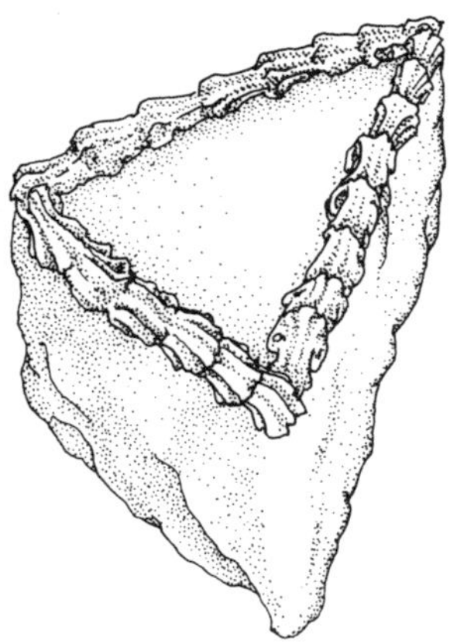

Decorate as follows with a small quantity of almond paste (see page 81), a small quantity of glacé icing tinted very lightly (see page 86) and a small quantity of vanilla-flavoured butter cream (see page 90).

Roll out the almond paste to a thickness of about 25 mm (⅛ inch). Cut out triangular- or diamond-shaped pieces to fit the tops of the sponges. Press into place. Cut out either three or four strips to fit the sides of the sponges and press into place on the sponges. Allow to dry out for 30 minutes.

Place the prepared sponges on a cooling rack, place a plate underneath and then spoon over the glacé icing to coat the entire sponges. Allow the icing to set, then decorate by piping a small border of butter cream along the top outside edge of the sponge.

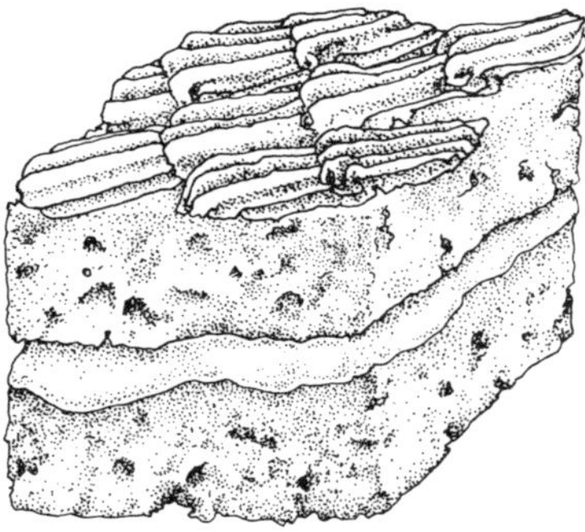

(3) Butter cream iced fancy: these look most attractive when made with contrasting colours of sponge, e.g. pale pink with pale green. Cut a strip of sponge 3.8 cm (1½ inches) wide. Cut in half through the middle. Spread one half with a little flavoured and/or tinted butter cream (see page 90) and sandwich together with the other half. Brush

the top with warmed apricot glaze (see page 93) and allow to set.

Decorate with a small quantity of butter cream in two contrasting colours. Pipe lines of butter cream along the length of the prepared sponge using alternating colours. Cut the iced sponge into diamond shapes 4.2 cm (1⅝ inches) along each side.

(4) Chocolate boxes: make a 3-egg Genoese sponge flavoured with chocolate (see page 32). Decorate with a small quantity of chocolate-flavoured butter cream (see page 90), and enough chocolate squares to cover the four sides of each sponge base cut out slightly larger than the prepared base.

Cut out the cold prepared sponge into the required number of cubes, about 4 cm (1½ inches) in size. Spread the four sides of each sponge with butter cream and place the chocolate squares in position. Pipe the top of each sponge with butter cream using a No. 6 star nozzle.

(5) Cauliflower cakes: make a basic Genoese sponge, baked in a slab (see page 32). Using a small, circular cutter about 2.5-4 cm (1-1½ inches) in diameter, cut out the required number of sponge bases. Brush with warmed apricot glaze (see page 93) and allow to set.

Decorate with a small quantity of almond paste (see page 81) tinted pale green and a small quantity of vanilla-flavoured butter cream (see page 90).

Roll out the almond paste very thinly. Cut into 4-cm (1½-inch) rounds allowing four rounds for each cake. Place these rounds, overlapping, around the sides of the cake, pressing the top edges slightly outwards. Using a small No. 6 star nozzle, pipe small stars of butter cream in the centre of each cake to resemble the curds of a cauliflower.

RASPBERRY MERINGUE GÂTEAU

Meringue
2 egg whites
100 g (4 oz) caster sugar

Sponge
2 egg yolks
50 g (2 oz) caster sugar
1 tbsp cold water
50 g (2 oz) plain flour

Filling
275 ml (½ pint) double or whipping cream
225 g (8 oz) fresh, frozen or canned raspberries, or canned apricots

Heat the oven to 110°C (225°F) mark ½. Line a large baking tray with non-stick parchment and mark out two 18-cm (7-inch) circles on the paper.

Whisk the egg whites until they form stiff peaks then whisk in 2 teaspoonfuls of the sugar; fold in the remaining sugar. Spread the meringue in the two 18-cm (7-inch) circles on the prepared tray. Place in the oven and bake for about 2 hours. Allow to cool on the tray, then remove to a cooling rack and carefully remove the lining paper.

To make the sponge, place the egg yolks and sugar in a mixing bowl and whisk until thick and creamy, then whisk in the water. Very lightly fold in the flour then place in an 18-cm (7-inch) greased and base-lined sandwich tin. Bake in a preheated oven at 180°C (350°F) mark 4 for 20 minutes until just firm to the touch. Allow to cool in the tin then turn out onto a cooling rack and remove the lining paper.

To assemble, whip the cream until it will just hold a soft peak and is of spreading consistency. If using frozen raspberries, thaw and retain any juices. Add a little sugar to sweeten. If using canned raspberries, strain, retaining the juices. (Canned apricots may be used as an alternative).

Place one meringue round on a serving dish; spread with one third of the cream. Place the sponge round on top and sprinkle with any retained juices. Arrange the raspberries on top and spread with half the remaining cream. Place the second meringue round on top, pressing lightly in place.

The remaining cream may be used to decorate either by spreading over or piping around the edge. When fresh raspberries are used, retain a few for decoration.

CHOCOLATE AND RUM GÂTEAU

75 g (3 oz) self-raising flour
25 g (1 oz) cocoa
4 eggs
100 g (4 oz) caster sugar
2 tbsp corn oil

Filling
150 g (5 oz) butter or margarine
225 g (8 oz) sieved icing sugar
3 tbsp rum (or brandy)

Icing
7 tbsp evaporated milk
1 tbsp rum (or brandy)
175 g (6 oz) plain chocolate

Decoration
coarsely grated chocolate

Heat the oven to 180°C (350°F) mark 4. Lightly grease and line a 20-cm (8-inch) round cake tin and lightly grease the lining paper. Sieve the flour with the cocoa.

Place the eggs and caster sugar in a mixing bowl and whisk until blended, then place over a pan of gently steaming water, making sure the bowl is not sitting in the water. Whisk until doubled in bulk, thick and creamy in consistency and leaving a distinct trail when the whisk is lifted out. Remove from the hot water and continue whisking until the mixture is cool and of the consistency of lightly whipped cream. Sieve the flour and cocoa into the bowl and fold in lightly, using the side of a metal spoon, then fold in the oil until evenly blended.

Place in the prepared tin and bake for about 45 minutes or until firm to the touch and beginning to shrink from the sides of the tin. Allow to cool in the tin for 3-4 minutes then turn out onto a cooling rack.

To make the filling, cream the butter or margarine until light in texture, then beat in the sieved icing sugar together with the rum.

For the icing, place the evaporated milk with the rum in a small saucepan and heat gently until the mixture is very hot but not boiling. Remove the pan from the heat and add the grated chocolate, stirring well until it is dissolved. Return the pan to the heat and cook gently, stirring continuously, until the icing just coats the back of a wooden spoon. Use at once. To assemble the gâteau, cut the sponge into four equal layers. Spread the three lower layers with the filling and reassemble the sponge. Place on a rack over a sheet of greaseproof paper; pour the chocolate icing over the top to cover it. Allow to firm up. Decorate with grated chocolate.

PRALINE GÂTEAU

1 recipe quantity Genoese sponge (see page 32)
2-egg-white quantity of crème au beurre à meringue (see page 92)
50 g (2 oz) praline (see page 89)
1/2 recipe quantity caramel (see page 92)
50 g (2 oz) browned flaked almonds

Make up the Genoese sponge. Make the crème au beurre à meringue and beat in the powdered praline. Make the caramel and break into small pieces.

Cut the sponge in half and sandwich together with one third of the crème au beurre. Spread another third of the crème over the sides and top of the sponge. Coat the sides of the sponge with the browned flaked almonds.

Place the remaining crème au beurre in a forcing bag fitted with a No. 6 star nozzle. Mark the surface of the sponge into 8 sections and pipe with crème au beurre then decorate alternate sections with the small pieces of caramel. Finally pipe the remaining crème au beurre in a decorative pattern around the edge of the sponge.

MOCHA GÂTEAU

1 recipe quantity Genoese sponge flavoured with 2 tsp coffee essence (see page 32)
2-egg-white quantity of crème au beurre à meringue flavoured with 2-3 tsp coffee essence (see page 92)
50-75 g (2-3 oz) coarsely grated chocolate or chocolate vermicelli
8 chocolate triangles (see page 15)

Cut the sponge in half and sandwich together with a quarter of the crème au beurre. Spread another quarter of the crème over the sides and top of the sponge then coat the sides with either the grated chocolate or the chocolate vermicelli.

Place the remaining crème au beurre in a forcing bag fitted with a No. 6 star nozzle. Mark the surface of the sponge into 8 sections and outline each section with a line or twisted 'rope' of crème, increasing your pressure on the forcing bag as you pipe towards the outside edge of the sponge. This will result in a deeper line or 'rope' of crème at the edge. Arrange the chocolate triangles at a slight angle along the piped design, radiating out from the centre of the sponge.

CHOCOLATE CREAM SWISS ROLL

65 g (2½ oz) plain flour
15 g (½ oz) cocoa
½ tsp baking powder
3 eggs
90 g (3½ oz) caster sugar

Filling
75 g (3 oz) butter
115 g (4½ oz) icing sugar
40 g (1½ oz) ground almonds
a few drops of vanilla flavouring

Heat the oven to 200°C (400°F) mark 6. Grease and line a 33 × 23-cm (13 × 9-inch) Swiss roll tin and lightly grease the lining paper. Sieve the flour with the cocoa and baking powder.

Place the eggs with the sugar in a roomy, heat-resistant bowl and place over a pan of gently steaming water, making sure the bottom of the bowl is not touching the water. Whisk until the mixture thickens and the whisk leaves a trail when lifted out. Remove from the hot water and continue whisking until the mixture has cooled. Lightly fold in the sieved flour mixture and place in the prepared tin, smoothing the mixture well into the corners. Bake for about 10 minutes or until firm to the touch and beginning to shrink from the sides of the tin.

Turn out quickly onto a sheet of lightly sugared greaseproof paper, remove the lining paper, trim off the outside edges of the sponge, then immediately replace the tin on top. Cover with a damp cloth and leave to become quite cold.

For the filling, cream the butter until light and fluffy, then add the sieved icing sugar a little at a time together with the ground almonds and vanilla flavouring. Beat well, then spread the filling evenly over the cold Swiss roll to within 5 mm (¼ inch) of the edge. Roll up firmly from the short edge and remove from the greaseproof paper.

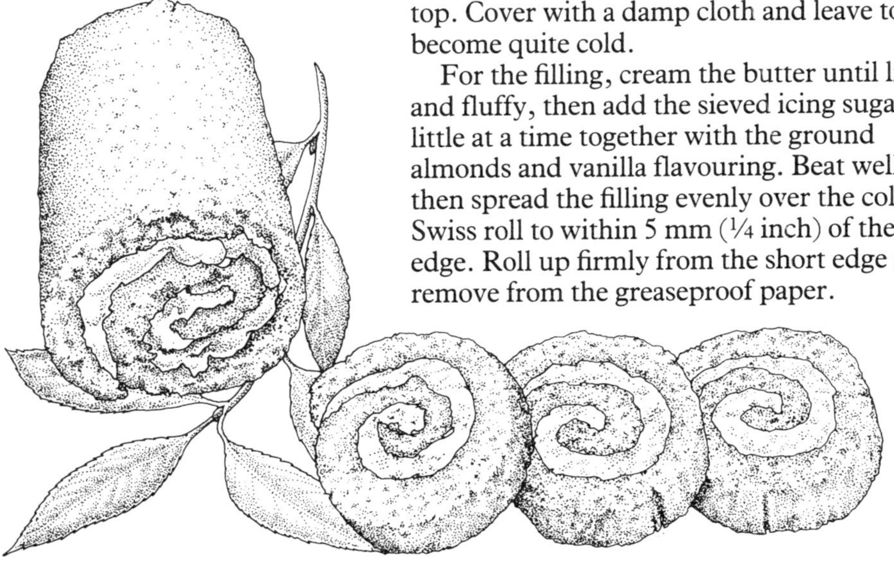

RICH CAKES

This chapter contains a variety of recipes for both large and small cakes which keep well. Included are the traditional special occasion cakes as well as some interesting old-fashioned recipes. They are made by the creaming method and, in some instances, are iced and decorated. For successful results, make sure all ingredients are at room temperature.

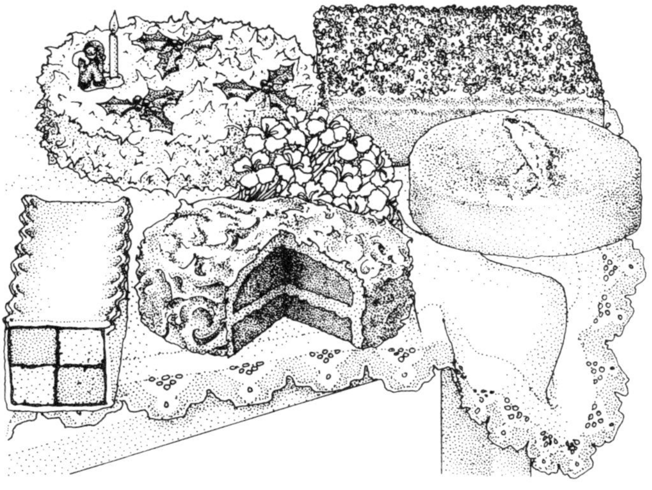

APPLE COURTING CAKES

Filling
450 g (1 lb) cooking apples
3 tbsp water

Pastry
175 g (6 oz) plain flour
pinch of salt
40 g (1½ oz) margarine
40 g (1½ oz) lard
about 6 tsp water

Topping
75 g (3 oz) margarine
75 g (3 oz) caster sugar
2 eggs
175 g (6 oz) self-raising flour

Icing
75 g (3 oz) margarine
finely grated zest of ½ lemon
175 g (6 oz) icing sugar
2 tsp lemon juice

Prepare the apple filling by peeling, coring and slicing the apples into a saucepan; add the water. Place the lid on the pan and cook the apples over a very low heat until they begin to break up. Mash with a wooden spoon until the apples are cooked and smooth in consistency. Remove the apple purée from the pan and leave to cool.

To make the pastry, sieve the flour with the salt; blend the fats together then rub into the flour until the mixture resembles fine breadcrumbs. Add the water and mix to form a firm, but not crumbly, pastry. Knead lightly to remove any cracks, then place the pastry in a polythene bag and refrigerate for 30 minutes.

Heat the oven to 190°C (375°F) mark 5. Roll out the pastry to a rectangle about 30 × 23 cm (12 × 9 inches) and use to line a Swiss roll tin 28 × 20 cm (11 × 8 inches). Trim the edges. Spread with the cold apple purée.

For the topping, cream the margarine with the caster sugar until the mixture is light and creamy. Whisk the eggs and beat into the mixture. Sieve the flour, then fold into the mixture to form a soft dropping consistency. Place spoonfuls of the cake mixture over the apple, then spread lightly to cover.

Bake for about 30 minutes until golden and firm to the touch. Leave to cool in the tin.

To make the icing, cream the margarine until light in consistency, then add the lemon zest. Sieve the icing sugar then beat into the margarine with the lemon juice. Spread the icing over the cooked, cold cake, then cut into fingers.

GINGER MARMALADE CAKE

100 g (4 oz) margarine
100 g (4 oz) caster sugar
2 eggs
225 g (8 oz) self-raising flour
1 tsp ground ginger
4 tbsp ginger marmalade
3 tbsp milk

Heat the oven to 180°C (350°F) mark 4. Grease and line an 18-cm (7-inch) round cake tin and grease the lining paper.

Cream the margarine and sugar together until light and fluffy. Whisk the eggs lightly and beat into the creamed mixture. Sieve the flour and ground ginger, fold lightly into the creamed mixture and then fold in the marmalade. Add the milk to give a soft dropping consistency.

Place in the prepared tin and smooth over the top. Bake for 45 minutes then reduce the oven temperature to 170°C (325°F) mark 3 and continue baking for another 15 minutes or until firm to the touch and beginning to shrink from the sides of the tin.

Leave to cool in the tin for 15-20 minutes then turn onto a cooling rack.

CHOCOLATE BROWNIES

75 g (3 oz) walnuts
50 g (2 oz) plain chocolate
100 g (4 oz) plain flour
pinch of salt
¾ tsp baking powder
75 g (3 oz) margarine
50 g (2 oz) caster sugar
1 egg
a little milk to mix
a little caster sugar for dredging

Set the oven to 180°C (350°F) mark 4. Lightly grease an 18-cm (7-inch) square cake tin.

Chop the walnuts roughly; grate the chocolate into a small basin and suspend the basin over a pan of gently steaming water until the chocolate has melted, stirring occasionally. Sieve the flour, salt and baking powder.

Cream the margarine with the caster sugar until light and creamy. Whisk the egg lightly, beat into the creamed mixture, then stir in the melted chocolate. Lightly fold in the flour then fold in the walnuts. Add sufficient milk to give a soft dropping consistency. Place in the prepared tin, smooth over the top, hollowing out the centre a little. Dredge lightly with caster sugar.

Bake for 30-35 minutes or until firm to the touch and beginning to shrink from the sides of the tin. Cut into squares while the cake is still warm, then leave to cool in the tin before turning out onto a cooling rack.

MADEIRA CAKE

225 g (8 oz) butter or margarine
225 g (8 oz) caster sugar
5 eggs
zest of 1 lemon
250 g (9 oz) plain flour
a little finely sliced citron peel

Heat the oven to 180°C (350°F) mark 4. Lightly grease and line a 18-cm (7-inch) round cake tin and lightly grease the lining paper. Cream the butter or margarine and caster sugar until the mixture is light and creamy. Lightly beat the eggs and mix in the lemon zest. Beat the eggs into the creamed mixture, adding sufficient flour to prevent curdling. Fold in the remaining flour.

Place in the prepared tin, smooth over the top and hollow out the centre a little. Bake for 30 minutes and, without removing from the oven, quickly decorate with the citron peel. Reduce the oven temperature to 170°C (325°F) mark 3 and cook for a further 45-60 minutes or until the cake is golden in colour, firm to the touch and beginning to shrink from the sides of the tin.

Cool in the tin for 10 minutes then turn out onto a cooling rack.

FORFAR FRUIT CAKE

225 g (8 oz) currants
225 g (8 oz) sultanas
50 g (2 oz) glacé cherries
50 g (2 oz) walnuts
225 g (8 oz) plain flour
pinch of salt
2 tsp baking powder
200 g (7 oz) wholemeal flour
150 g (5 oz) butter and 150 g (5 oz) margarine, mixed
275 g (10 oz) caster sugar
3 eggs
3 tbsp milk

Heat the oven to 170°C (325°F) mark 3. Lightly grease and line a 20-cm (8-inch) round cake tin and grease the lining paper.

Wash the currants and sultanas; dry thoroughly. Wash and quarter the glacé cherries; dry well. Roughly chop the walnuts. Sieve the plain white flour with the salt and baking powder and mix with the wholemeal flour.

Cream the butter and margarine with the caster sugar until light and fluffy. Whisk the eggs lightly and beat into the creamed mixture, alternating with the flour. Stir in the prepared fruit and nuts, then add sufficient milk to give a soft dropping consistency. Mix well but lightly.

Place in the prepared tin, hollowing out the centre a little. Bake for 1 hour then reduce the oven temperature to 150°C (300°F) mark 2 and bake for a further 45-60 minutes or until firm to the touch and beginning to shrink from the sides of the tin.

Allow to cool in the tin for 15 minutes, then turn out onto a cooling rack.

MADELEINES

100 g (4 oz) margarine
100 g (4 oz) caster sugar
2 eggs
100 g (4 oz) self-raising flour

Decoration
raspberry or apricot jam
fine-grain desiccated coconut
glacé cherries and angelica

Heat the oven to 190°C (375°F) mark 5. Lightly grease 12-15 dariole moulds.

Cream the margarine and caster sugar together until light and fluffy. Whisk the eggs and add them, a little at a time, to the creamed mixture, beating well. Very lightly fold in the sieved flour to give a soft dropping consistency. Add a little hot water if necessary.

Half fill the prepared moulds and bake for about 12-15 minutes or until golden, firm to

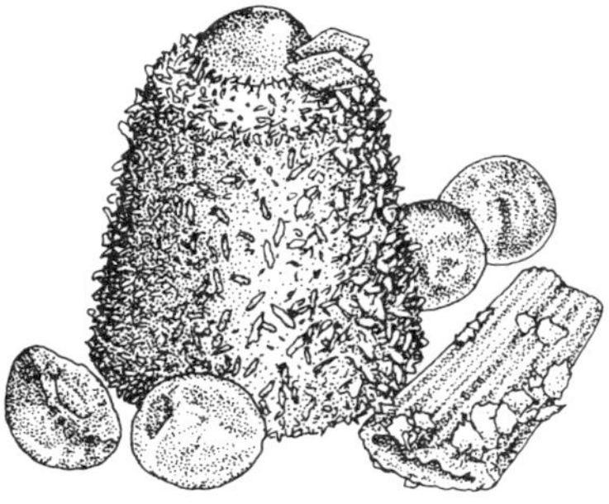

the touch and beginning to shrink from the sides of the moulds. Leave to cool for 5 minutes then turn out onto a cooling rack.

Warm the jam. Trim the base of each cake so it will stand upright without toppling. Brush with the warmed jam and roll in desiccated coconut. Wash the cherries and angelica. Halve the cherries, cut small diamond shapes from a strip of angelica and use to decorate the top of each madeleine.

CARROT CAKE

50 g (2 oz) raisins
175 g (6 oz) margarine
75 g (3 oz) brown sugar
2 eggs
275 g (10 oz) self-raising wholemeal flour (or white flour, if preferred)
1/2 tsp ground cinnamon
25 g (1 oz) mixed peel or marmalade
finely grated zest of 1 orange
225 g (8 oz) finely grated carrot
milk to mix

Heat the oven to 180°C (350°F) mark 4. Lightly grease an 18-cm (7-inch) square or a 20-cm (8-inch) round cake tin. Wash the raisins.

Cream the margarine with the sugar until light and creamy. Whisk the eggs and beat into the mixture. Sieve the flour with the cinnamon (ensuring any residue from the wholemeal flour is added to the bowl). Fold into the creamed mixture together with the peel or marmalade, orange zest and raisins.

Mix in the grated carrots. Add sufficient milk to give a soft dropping consistency (wholemeal flour will require more milk than white flour).

Place in the prepared tin and smooth over the top, hollowing out the centre a little.

Bake for 40 minutes then reduce the oven temperature to 170°C (325°F) mark 3 and bake for a further 40-50 minutes until firm to the touch and beginning to shrink from the sides of the tin.

Cool in the tin for 15 minutes, then turn out onto a cooling rack.

SPICED APPLE CAKE

450 g (1 lb) mixed dried fruit
50 g (2 oz) walnuts
225 g (8 oz) plain flour
1 tsp cinnamon
½ tsp mixed spice
½ tsp ground ginger
1 tsp bicarbonate of soda
150 g (5 oz) margarine
175 g (6 oz) dark soft brown sugar
2 eggs
finely grated zest of ½ lemon
275 ml (½ pint) apple pulp
a little granulated sugar

Wash the dried fruit and dry thoroughly; roughly chop the walnuts. Sieve the flour, spices and bicarbonate of soda together.

Lightly grease and line a 20-cm (8-inch) square cake tin and grease the lining paper. Heat the oven to 180°C (350°F) mark 4.

Cream together the margarine and sugar until light and creamy. Whisk the eggs lightly and beat into the creamed mixture. Carefully fold in the flour then add the prepared fruit and nuts. Mix well. Fold in the lemon zest and apple pulp.

Place in the prepared tin, smooth over the top and sprinkle with the granulated sugar.

Bake for 1 hour then cover the top of the cake with a sheet of greaseproof paper or foil and bake for a further 30 minutes or until the top is firm to the touch and the cake is beginning to shrink from the sides of the tin.

Allow to cool in the tin for 15 minutes then turn out onto a cooling rack.

CHOCOLATE ORANGE DRIZZLE CAKE

175 g (6 oz) margarine
175 (6 oz) caster sugar
3 eggs
finely grated zest of 2 oranges
175 g (6 oz) self-raising flour
milk to mix

Orange syrup
juice of 2 oranges
50 g (2 oz) granulated sugar

Icing
100 g (4 oz) plain chocolate
15 g (½ oz) margarine or butter

Heat the oven to 180°C (350°F) mark 4. Lightly grease and line a 900-g (2-lb) loaf tin and grease the lining paper.

Cream the margarine and caster sugar together until light and creamy. Lightly beat the eggs and beat into the mixture together with the orange zest. Sieve the flour and fold lightly into the creamed mixture. Add a little milk to give a soft dropping consistency. Place in the prepared tin and smooth over the top, hollowing out the centre a little.

Bake for 1-1¼ hours or until well risen, firm to the touch and beginning to shrink from the sides of the tin. Allow to cool in the tin for 5 minutes then turn out onto a cooling rack.

For the orange syrup, strain the orange juice and warm gently in a saucepan with the sugar until the sugar has dissolved.

To make the icing, grate the chocolate into a small basin and suspend over a saucepan of gently simmering water. Stir occasionally until the chocolate is melted and smooth.

When the cake is almost cold, make a series of shallow cuts across the top of it, about 2 cm (¾ inch) apart, then "drizzle" the prepared orange syrup over the top so that it soaks into the cake. Stir the margarine into the warm, melted chocolate until it is thoroughly mixed in. Spread or swirl the icing over the top of the cake.

LEMON CAKE

175 g (6 oz) margarine
175 g (6 oz) caster sugar
2 eggs
4 tbsp milk
175 g (6 oz) self-raising flour
finely grated zest and juice of 1 large lemon
1 tbsp icing sugar

Heat the oven to 180°C (350°F) mark 4. Lightly grease and line a 900-g (2-lb) loaf tin.

Cream the margarine and caster sugar together until light and creamy, then gradually beat in the lightly whisked eggs together with the milk. Lightly fold in the sieved flour and lemon zest.

Place in the prepared tin and smooth over the top. Bake for 30 minutes then reduce the oven temperature to 170°C (325°F) mark 3 for a further 30 minutes or until the cake is golden brown, firm to the touch and beginning to shrink from the sides of the tin.

Mix the lemon juice with the icing sugar and pour over the cake as soon as it has been taken out of the oven. Allow the glaze to set, then remove the cake from the tin and place on a cooling rack.

SANDWICH CAKE AND SMALL CAKES

175 g (6 oz) margarine
175 g (6 oz) caster sugar
3 eggs
175 g (6 oz) self-raising flour
a few drops of vanilla flavouring
1 tbsp hot water

Heat the oven to 180°C (350°F) mark 4. Lightly grease and line the bases of two 18-cm (7-inch) sandwich cake tins and grease the lining paper.

Cream the margarine and sugar together until light and fluffy. Lightly whisk the eggs and add, a little at a time, to the creamed mixture, beating well. If the mixture shows signs of curdling, add a little sieved flour. Add the vanilla flavouring. Lightly fold in the remaining sieved flour then add the hot water carefully. Mix evenly to give a soft dropping consistency. If necessary add a little more water.)

Divide evenly between the tins, smooth over the top and bake for about 20-25 minutes until golden in colour, firm to the touch and beginning to shrink from the sides of the tins. Leave to cool in the tins for 3-4 minutes then turn out onto a rack.

When cold, sandwich together with the chosen filling. Dust with a little caster sugar. Alternatively, these cakes may be filled with butter cream (see page 90), in which case, dust with a little sieved icing sugar.

Sandwich cakes may, with the exception of

a Victoria Sandwich cake, be iced and decorated using any simple icing like glacé icing, quick frostings, fudge icings, butter creams, etc. (see chapter 6). The sides of the cake may be coated with icing etc., although not for show purposes as they are then classified as gâteaux and not sandwich cakes.

Variations

(1) Victoria sandwich cake: fill with raspberry jam (homemade if possible).
(2) Lemon sandwich cake: add the finely grated zest of 1 lemon to the mixture and fill with lemon curd.
(3) Orange sandwich cake: add the finely grated zest of 1 orange to the mixture and fill with either orange curd or butter cream (see page 90) flavoured with orange juice.
(4) Coffee sandwich cake: add 3 teaspoonfuls coffee essence to the mixture and fill with coffee butter cream (see page 90).
(5) Chocolate sandwich cake: replace 1 tablespoonful flour with 1 tablespoonful cocoa and add ½ tablespoonful golden syrup to the creamed mixture before adding the flour. Fill with vanilla-flavoured butter cream or with chocolate-flavoured butter cream (see page 90).
(6) Small cakes: the basic sandwich cake mixture may be made into small cakes, either baking them in bun tins or in paper cases. These small cakes may be iced and decorated as desired, (see chapter 6).
(7) Butterfly cakes: bake in paper cases; when cold, cut a slice from the top of each cake and cut this slice in half. Spread or pipe a little butter cream (see page 90) on the top of the cake; place the two halves in position to form wings. Lightly dredge with sieved icing sugar before serving.

CHERRY AND ALMOND CAKE

100 g (4 oz) glacé cherries
100 g (4 oz) butter
100 g (4 oz) margarine
225 g (8 oz) caster sugar
3 eggs
¼ tsp almond essence
225 g (8 oz) plain flour
100 g (4 oz) ground almonds
1 tsp baking powder
a little granulated sugar for sprinkling

Heat the oven to 140°C (275°F) mark 1. Grease a 20-cm (8-inch) round cake tin and line the base and sides with doubled greaseproof paper. Brush the lining paper with melted fat.

Halve, wash and dry the cherries. Cream the butter, margarine and caster sugar together until light and fluffy. Beat the eggs and almond essence together and add gradually, beating well after each addition. Add the cherries and mix thoroughly.

Sieve together the flour, ground almonds and baking powder and fold very lightly into the creamed mixture. Place in the prepared tin and smooth over the top. Sprinkle the granulated sugar over the top.

Bake for 2¼ hours or until the cake is starting to shrink from the sides of the tin and is firm to the touch.

Cool for 15 minutes in the tin before turning out onto a cooling rack.

DUNDEE CAKE

350 g (12 oz) plain flour
1 tsp baking powder
1 tsp mixed spice
400 g (14 oz) mixed dried fruit
225 g (8 oz) butter or margarine
225 g (8 oz) caster sugar
4 eggs
100 g (4 oz) chopped mixed peel
25 g (1 oz) blanched halved almonds

Heat the oven to 170°C (325°F) mark 3. Lightly grease and line a 20-cm (8-inch) round cake tin and grease the lining paper.

Sieve the flour, baking powder and spice. Wash the dried fruit and dry thoroughly.

Cream the butter or margarine with the caster sugar until light and fluffy. Whisk the eggs lightly then beat into the creamed mixture, alternating with a little of the flour. Fold in the remaining flour together with the prepared fruit and peel.

Place in the prepared tin; smooth over the top. Place halved almonds, round side uppermost, in a neat pattern on top. Bake for about 2½ hours or until golden in colour, firm to the touch and beginning to shrink from the sides of the tin. (It may be necessary to cover the cake with a piece of foil or greaseproof paper half-way through cooking to avoid the cake becoming too brown.)

Leave to cool in the tin for 15-20 minutes, then turn out onto a cooling rack.

COFFEE ALMOND CAKE

100 g (4 oz) butter or margarine
100 (4 oz) caster sugar
2 eggs
2 tbsp liquid coffee essence
3 tbsp sherry
150 g (5 oz) self-raising flour
50 g (2 oz) ground almonds
15 g (½ oz) chopped almonds

Heat the oven to 170°C (325°F) mark 3. Lightly grease and line a 15-cm (6-inch) round cake tin then grease the lining.

Cream the butter or margarine with the caster sugar until light and creamy, then beat in the lightly whisked eggs, coffee essence and 1 tablespoonful of the sherry, alternating with a little sifted flour. Fold in the remaining flour and ground almonds.

Place in the prepared tin, smooth over the top, hollowing out the centre a little. Sprinkle with the chopped almonds and bake for about 1 hour, then reduce the oven temperature to 150°C (300°F) mark 2 and bake for a further 30 minutes or until firm to the touch and beginning to shrink from the sides of the tin.

Leave to cool in the tin for 15 minutes then turn out onto a cooling rack.

When the cake is cold, remove the lining paper, prick the base with a fork and pour over the remaining sherry. Ideally, keep the cake for a week before eating.

YUM YUM CAKES

50 g (2 oz) caster sugar
100 g (4 oz) margarine
2 egg yolks
finely grated zest and juice of 1/2 lemon
175 g (6 oz) self-raising flour

Topping
25 g (1 oz) walnuts
25 g (1 oz) glacé cherries
2 egg whites
100 g (4 oz) caster sugar

Heat the oven to 180°C (350°F) mark 4. Grease and line a 28 × 20-cm (11 × 8-inch) Swiss roll tin and grease the lining paper.

Cream the margarine and sugar together until light and creamy, then beat in the egg yolks and lemon zest. Fold in the flour, together with the lemon juice. Spread in the prepared tin in an even layer.

For the topping, roughly chop the walnuts and finely chop the glacé cherries. Whisk the egg whites until they form stiff peaks, then beat in the sugar a little at a time. Fold in the prepared nuts and cherries. Spread over the cake base, ensuring that the meringue reaches well into the corners of the tin.

Bake for 20-25 minutes until golden. Leave to cool for a few minutes, then, with a sharp knife, cut into fingers or squares, dipping the knife in cold water between each cut. Leave to cool in the tin.

DEVIL'S FOOD CAKE

50 g (2 oz) cocoa
200 ml (7 fl oz) warm water
100 g (4 oz) margarine
275 g (10 oz) caster sugar
2 eggs
175 g (6 oz) plain flour
1/4 tsp baking powder
1 tsp bicarbonate of soda

Icing
100 g (4 oz) soft margarine
75 g (3 oz) granulated sugar
4 tbsp milk
1 tsp coffee essence
225 g (8 oz) icing sugar
2 tbsp cocoa

Heat the oven to 180°C (350°F) mark 4. Lightly grease and line the base of two 20-cm (8-inch) sandwich tins. Grease the lining paper.

Blend the cocoa with the water and allow to cool. Place the margarine and caster sugar in a mixing bowl and cream together until light and fluffy. Lightly whisk the eggs and beat into the creamed mixture.

Sieve the flour with the baking powder and bicarbonate of soda and lightly fold into the creamed mixture together with the cooled cocoa mixture.

Place in the tins. Smooth over the top. Bake for 40-45 minutes or until firm to the

touch and beginning to shrink from the sides of the tins. Allow to cool in the tins for 4-5 minutes then turn out onto a cooling rack.

To make the icing, melt the margarine in a small saucepan, then stir in the granulated sugar, milk and coffee essence. Bring slowly to the boil, stirring continuously, ensuring the sugar is fully dissolved before the mixture comes to the boil. Put aside to cool slightly.

Sieve the icing sugar and cocoa into a mixing bowl. Stir in the cooled liquid and beat well until cooled to a coating or spreading consistency, as desired. Fill and ice the cakes with the prepared icing.

RUM AND ORANGE CAKE

finely grated zest and juice of 1 large orange
3 tbsp rum
175 g (6 oz) margarine
175 g (6 oz) caster sugar
3 eggs
225 g (8 oz) plain flour
1½ tsp baking powder

Grease and line an 18-cm (7-inch) round tin. Place the orange zest and juice in a small basin with the rum. Leave overnight.

Heat the oven to 170°C (325°F) mark 3. Cream the margarine and caster sugar until light and fluffy. Separate the eggs, placing the egg whites in a large bowl. Add the egg yolks to the creamed mixture, beating well. Sieve the flour with the baking powder then fold into the creamed mixture adding a little of the orange and rum mixture between each addition of flour.

Whisk the egg whites until they form soft peaks then fold very lightly into the mixture. Place in the prepared tin and smooth over the top.

Bake for 1½ hours until golden in colour, firm to the touch and beginning to shrink from the sides of the tin. Leave to cool in the tin for 10 minutes then turn out onto a cooling rack.

GOLDEN HARVEST CAKE

175 g (6 oz) sultanas
25 g (1 oz) walnuts
175 g (6 oz) margarine
100 g (4 oz) caster sugar
50 g (2 oz) clear honey
3 eggs
225 g (8 oz) self-raising flour (wholemeal or white)
finely grated zest of 1 large orange
3-4 tbsp orange juice

Heat the oven to 170°C (325°F) mark 3. Lightly grease and line an 18-cm (7-inch) round cake tin and grease the lining paper.

Wash the sultanas and dry thoroughly; roughly chop the walnuts.

Cream the margarine and caster sugar together until light and fluffy then beat in the honey. Whisk the eggs and beat into the creamed mixture adding a little sieved flour to prevent any curdling. Stir in the prepared sultanas, walnuts and orange zest, then fold in the remaining flour. Add sufficient orange juice to give a soft dropping consistency.

Place in the prepared tin, smooth over the top then bake for 1¼-1½ hours or until golden in colour, firm to the touch and beginning to shrink from the sides of the tin.

Leave to cool in the tin for 10 minutes then turn out onto a cooling rack.

PARADISE CAKE

350 g (12 oz) sultanas
225 g (8 oz) glacé cherries
175 g (6 oz) glacé pineapple
50 g (2 oz) angelica
50 g (2 oz) walnuts
225 g (8 oz) plain flour
100 g (4 oz) self-raising flour
350 g (12 oz) butter or margarine
225 g (8 oz) caster sugar
5 eggs
50 g (2 oz) mixed peel
finely grated zest and juice of 1 lemon
8 tbsp milk or sherry

Wash the sultanas, glacé cherries, glacé pineapple and angelica and dry thoroughly. Finely chop the cherries, pineapple and angelica and roughly chop the walnuts. Sieve the flours together.

Heat the oven to 170°C (325°F) mark 3. Lightly grease and line a 20-cm (8-inch) round cake tin and grease the lining paper.

Cream the butter or margarine with the caster sugar until it is light and creamy. Lightly whisk the eggs and beat into the creamed mixture, adding a little flour to prevent the mixture curdling. Fold in the remaining flour with the prepared fruit, peel and nuts. Mix thoroughly then add the lemon zest, lemon juice and the milk or sherry to give a soft dropping consistency. Place in the prepared tin and smooth over the top, hollowing out the centre a little.

Bake for 1½ hours then reduce the oven temperature to 150°C (300°F) mark 2. Cover the top of the cake with a sheet of greaseproof paper or foil to avoid over-browning, then bake for a further 1½-2 hours or until the cake is firm to the touch and beginning to shrink from the sides of the tin.

Leave to cool in the tin for 30 minutes then turn out onto a cooling rack.

RICH ALMOND CAKE

100 g (4 oz) butter or margarine
150 g (5 oz) caster sugar
3 eggs
75 g (3 oz) ground almonds
40 g (1½ oz) plain flour
2-3 drops almond essence
extra caster sugar for dredging

Heat the oven to 180°C (350°F) mark 4. Lightly grease and line a deep 18-cm (7-inch) sandwich cake tin and grease the lining paper.

Cream the butter or margarine until slack in consistency, then beat in the caster sugar a tablespoonful at a time. Beat thoroughly until light and fluffy. Add the eggs, one at a time, adding one third of the almonds with each egg. Beat well. Sieve the flour then fold in with the almond essence.

Place in the prepared tin and bake for 40-45 minutes or until golden in colour, firm to the touch and beginning to shrink from the sides of the tin.

Leave to cool in the tin for 5 minutes then turn out onto a cooling rack. Dredge with a little caster sugar before serving.

CHRISTMAS CAKE

350 g (12 oz) sultanas
350 g (12 oz) currants
175 g (6 oz) raisins
50 g (2 oz) mixed chopped peel
50 g (2 oz) glacé cherries
100 g (4 oz) self-raising flour
175 g (6 oz) plain flour
1/4 tsp salt
1/2 tsp mixed spice
1/4 tsp ground cinnamon
1/4 tsp ground nutmeg
225 g (8 oz) butter
225 g (8 oz) soft brown sugar
4 eggs (size 1)
1 tbsp black treacle
1/4 tsp almond essence
1/4 tsp vanilla flavouring
50 g (2 oz) ground almonds
50 g (2 oz) chopped, blanched almonds
finely grated zest of 1 lemon
3-4 tbsp sherry
3-4 tbsp sherry or brandy for soaking cake

Icing
675 g (1½ lb) almond paste (see page 81)
Royal icing made with 675 g (1½ lb) icing sugar and 3 egg whites (see page 84)
apricot glaze (see page 93)

Wash the dried fruit and dry thoroughly. Wash the glacé cherries then cut into quarters. Grease an 18-cm (7-inch) square or 20-cm (8-inch) round cake tin and line with a double thickness of greaseproof paper, ensuring sufficient depth at the sides of the tin – the paper should come 5 cm (2 inches) above the top of the tin. Grease the lining paper. Tie a double thickness of either brown paper or kitchen paper around the outside of the tin, again to come above the rim of the tin.

Sieve the flour with the salt and spices. Heat the oven to 150°C (300°F) mark 2. Cream the butter until softened, then beat in the soft brown sugar until the mixture is light and fluffy. Beat in the eggs, one at a time, adding a little of the flour and spice mixture between each addition of egg. Beat in the treacle, flavouring and essence.

Fold in the remaining flour, then fold in the fruit, peel, ground and chopped almonds, and lemon zest. Mix lightly but thoroughly. Add 3-4 tablespoonfuls sherry.

Place in the prepared tin, smooth over the top, then hollow out the centre. Bake for 2 hours then reduce the oven temperature to 140°C (275°F) mark 1 and bake for a further 1½-2 hours or until firm to the touch and beginning to shrink slightly from the sides of the tin. It may be necessary to cover the cake to prevent it from becoming too brown.

Leave the cake in the tin until it is cold, then turn out onto a cooling rack or working surface. Remove the lining paper, invert the cake and prick the base with a fine skewer. Spoon over 3-4 tablespoonfuls sherry or brandy. Allow to dry out for 1 hour, then wrap in greaseproof paper and overwrap in foil. Repeat the addition of sherry or brandy at monthly intervals, if stored for several months. To ice the cake, see pages 81 and 84.

GOLDEN CHRISTMAS CAKE

100 g (4 oz) crystallised pineapple
100 g (4 oz) glacé cherries
350 g (12 oz) golden sultanas
100 g (4 oz) chopped walnuts
175 g (6 oz) butter or margarine
175 g (6 oz) caster sugar
4 eggs
250 g (9 oz) self-raising flour
3 tbsp sherry or whisky

Heat the oven to 170°C (325°F) mark 3. Lightly grease and line a 18-cm (7-inch) square or 20-cm (8-inch) round cake tin and grease the lining paper.

Wash the pineapple, glacé cherries and sultanas and dry thoroughly. Roughly chop the walnuts, finely chop the prepared pineapple and cherries and mix well together.

Cream the butter or margarine and sugar until light and creamy. Whisk the eggs lightly and beat into the creamed mixture, adding a little of the flour to avoid curdling. Fold in the remaining flour, alternating with the sherry or whisky, then add the prepared fruit and nuts, mixing lightly but thoroughly.

Place in the prepared tin, smoothing over the top, then slightly hollowing out the centre. Bake for 1 hour then reduce the oven temperature to 150°C (300°F) mark 2 and bake for a further 1½-2 hours or until the cake is firm to the touch and beginning to shrink from the sides of the tin. Leave to cool in the tin for about 30 minutes then turn out onto a cooling rack.

This is a delicious cake which can be iced in the same way as the more traditional Christmas cake (see pages 81 and 84).

QUICK AND EASY CAKES

These are recipes to try out when time is short. They are all quickly prepared and simple to make. Some cakes are made by the melting method, some by the all-in-one or one-stage method, and some use vegetable oil instead of a solid fat.

CHOCOLATE ORANGE YOGHURT CAKE

225 g (8 oz) self-raising flour
5 tbsp cocoa
pinch of salt
½ tsp bicarbonate of soda
3 eggs
150 ml (¼ pint) sunflower or corn oil
150 ml (¼ pint) orange-flavoured yoghurt
4 tbsp golden syrup
175 g (6 oz) soft brown sugar
finely grated zest of 1 orange

Topping (optional)
fudge icing (see page 87) or quick frosting (see page 89)

Heat the oven to 170°C (325°F) mark 3. Lightly oil and line a 20-cm (8-inch) round cake tin and lightly oil the lining paper.

Sieve the flour, cocoa, salt and bicarbonate of soda into a mixing bowl. Whisk the eggs and mix with the oil, yoghurt, syrup, sugar and orange zest. Stir into the flour and beat well, making sure they are evenly blended.

Place in the prepared tin and bake for 1¼-1½ hours or until firm to the touch and beginning to shrink from the sides of the tin. Allow to cool in the tin then turn out onto a cooling tray. Remove the lining paper.

For the topping, if used, make up the chosen icing and swirl over the cake.

GINGER SLICE

350 g (12 oz) plain flour
100 g (4 oz) soft brown sugar
175 g (6 oz) butter or margarine

Icing
75 g (3 oz) margarine
175 g (6 oz) soft brown sugar
1 tsp ground ginger

Heat the oven to 180°C (350°F) mark 4. Lightly grease a 29 × 19-cm (11½ × 7½-inch) Swiss roll tin.

Place the flour and sugar in a bowl and mix together. Melt the margarine or butter and pour into the bowl, mixing well. Press the mixture in an even layer into the prepared tin. Bake for 20-25 minutes or until just firm to the touch.

For the icing, place the margarine, sugar and ginger in a small saucepan and heat gently, stirring continuously, until all the sugar is dissolved. Bring to the boil and *without stirring*, boil until the mixture leaves the sides of the pan. Remove from the heat and beat until it starts to thicken and lose its shine. Pour on top of the cooked, warm shortbread base and spread evenly. Allow to cool in the tin, then cut into fingers or squares.

FARMHOUSE CAKE

275 g (10 oz) mixed dried fruit
200 g (7 oz) plain flour or wholemeal flour
25 g (1 oz) cornflour
½ tsp baking powder
1 tsp mixed spice
pinch of salt
175 g (6 oz) soft brown sugar
50 g (2 oz) chopped mixed peel
50 g (2 oz) glacé cherries
3 eggs
1 tbsp milk
200 ml (7 fl oz) corn oil

Heat the oven to 150°C (300°F) mark 2. Lightly oil and line an 18-cm (7-inch) round cake tin and lightly oil the lining paper. Wash the dried fruit and dry well.

Sieve the flour, cornflour, baking powder, mixed spice and salt into a mixing bowl (if using the wholemeal flour add the residue in the sieve to the bowl). Stir in the sugar, prepared dried fruits, peeled and halved glacé cherries (if very sticky with syrup, wash and dry well). Whisk the eggs with the milk and oil and stir into the dry ingredients, beating well until evenly distributed.

Place in the prepared tin, smooth over the top and hollow out the centre a little. Bake for 1½-1¾ hours or until golden in colour, firm to the touch and beginning to shrink from the sides of the tin. It may be necessary to cover the cake with greaseproof paper or foil after 45 minutes to avoid the cake becoming too brown.

Allow to cool in the tin for 8-10 minutes then turn out onto a cooling tray and remove the lining paper.

CHOCOLATE FINGERS

150 g (5 oz) self-raising flour
2 tbsp cocoa
100 g (4 oz) margarine
100 g (4 oz) caster sugar
50 g (2 oz) chopped dates
50 g (2 oz) chopped walnuts
1 egg
½ tsp vanilla flavouring
chocolate glacé icing (see page 86)

Heat the oven to 180°C (350°F) mark 4. Grease a shallow 18-cm (7-inch) square cake tin. Sieve the flour with the cocoa.

Place the margarine and sugar in a small saucepan and heat gently until the margarine is melted and the sugar dissolved. Place the sieved flour, the dates and nuts in a mixing bowl; make a well in the centre and pour in the melted mixture. Whisk the egg lightly with the vanilla flavouring and beat into the dry ingredients until well blended.

Place in the prepared tin, smooth over the top and bake for 25-30 minutes or until firm to the touch and beginning to shrink from the sides of the tin. Allow to cool in the tin then cut into fingers or squares.

Either ice with chocolate glacé icing (see page 86) before cutting into fingers or simply dust with sieved icing sugar before serving.

APPLE CAKE

675 g (1½ lb) mixed dried fruit
450 g (1 lb) cooking apples, peeled and cored
225 g (8 oz) margarine
225 g (8 oz) caster sugar
350 g (12 oz) plain flour
2 tsp bicarbonate of soda
2 tsp mixed spice
2 tsp ground cinnamon
2 eggs

Heat the oven to 170°C (325°F) mark 3. Lightly grease and line a 20-cm (8-inch) round cake tin and lightly grease the lining paper. Wash the dried fruit and dry well.

Slice the apples finely into a heavy-based saucepan; cover with the lid. Cook over a gentle heat without adding water and stir frequently (to prevent the apples burning) until the apples are reduced to a pulp. Beat with a wooden spoon until a purée is formed, then add the margarine to the pan together with the sugar. Stir well until melted then allow to cool.

Sieve the flour with the bicarbonate of soda and spices. Beat the eggs lightly and mix into the apple mixture. Fold in the flour until thoroughly and evenly blended. Add the prepared dried fruit and mix well.

Place in the prepared tin, smooth over the top and bake for 1 hour then reduce the oven temperature to 150°C (300°F) mark 2, cover the cake with greaseproof paper and continue to cook for a further 1¼-1½ hours or until firm to the touch and beginning to shrink from the sides of the tin. Allow to cool in the tin for 15 minutes then turn out onto a cooling rack and remove the lining paper.

BIRTHDAY CAKE

250 g (9 oz) plain flour
¼ tsp salt
2 tsp baking powder
1 tsp mixed spice
½ tsp ground cinnamon
½ tsp ground nutmeg
225 g (8 oz) currants
225 g (8 oz) sultanas
225 g (8 oz) raisins
100 g (4 oz) glacé cherries
225 g (8 oz) soft margarine
225 g (8 oz) soft brown sugar
5 eggs
1 tbsp black treacle
100 g (4 oz) chopped mixed peel
finely grated zest of 1 lemon
finely grated zest of 1 orange
1 tbsp lemon juice
2 tbsp sherry
50 g (2 oz) ground almonds
50 g (2 oz) chopped, blanched almonds

Heat the oven to 150°C (300°F) mark 2. Grease and line with doubled greaseproof paper a 20-cm (8-inch) square or a 23-cm (9-inch) round cake tin. Place a double thickness of either brown paper or kitchen paper around the outside of the tin to protect the sides of the cake during cooking.

Sieve the flour with the salt, baking powder and spices. Wash the dried fruit and quarter and wash the glacé cherries; dry thoroughly.

Place all the ingredients in a mixing bowl and beat together until well blended. Place in the prepared tin and hollow out the centre a little.

Bake for 1 hour then reduce the oven temperature to 140°C (275°F) mark 1 and continue to cook for a further 3-3½ hours or until firm to the touch and beginning to shrink slightly from the sides of the tin. It may be necessary to place a sheet of foil or greaseproof paper over the cake to prevent over-browning.

Leave in the tin until cold then turn out. Wrap in greaseproof paper and foil, store to mature the cake, then ice or use as desired.

WHOLEMEAL AND HONEY FRUIT CAKE

450 g (1 lb) mixed dried fruit
225 g (8 oz) wholemeal flour
1½ tsp bicarbonate of soda
1 tsp mixed spice
1 tsp ground cinnamon
½ tsp ground nutmeg
2 eggs
6 tbsp corn oil
200 ml (7 fl oz) milk
225 g (8 oz) clear honey

Heat the oven to 150°C (300°F) mark 2. Lightly oil and line an 18-cm (7-inch) square or 20-cm (8-inch) round cake tin and lightly oil the lining paper.

Wash the dried fruit and dry thoroughly. Sieve the flour with the bicarbonate of soda and spices, adding the residue in the sieve to the bowl. Stir in the prepared fruit and mix well. Whisk the eggs with the oil and the milk then add to the dry ingredients together with the honey. Mix thoroughly so the ingredients are well blended.

Place in the prepared tin and bake for 1¼-1½ hours or until golden, firm to the touch and beginning to shrink from the sides of the tin. Allow to cool in the tin for 8-10 minutes then turn out onto a cooling rack. Remove the lining paper.

SWISS ROLL

3 eggs
75 g (3 oz) caster sugar
75 g (3 oz) plain flour
3 tbsp vegetable oil

Topping and filling
a little caster sugar
3-4 tbsp jam

Lightly oil a 33 × 23-cm (13 × 9-inch) Swiss roll tin and line with greaseproof paper to come about 2.5 cm (1 inch) above the rim of the tin. Lightly oil the paper. Heat the oven to 220°C (425°F) mark 7.

Place the eggs and sugar in a deep, roomy mixing bowl and place over the pan of gently steaming water, ensuring that the base of the bowl is above the level of the water. Whisk together until thick and creamy in consistency and the mixture will hold a definite trail when the whisk is removed. Remove from the heat and continue whisking until the mixture cools. Sieve the flour and fold in very lightly using a spatula or the side of a metal spoon. Finally fold in the oil.

Place in the prepared tin, smoothing the mixture well into the corners of the tin. Bake for 8-10 minutes or until golden in colour, firm to the touch and beginning to shrink from the sides of the tin. Turn out at once onto greaseproof paper dredged with caster sugar. Trim the edges with a sharp knife, spread with warmed jam and roll up immediately. This cake stays moist and is easy to roll up.

CHOCOLATE GENOESE SPONGE

100 g (4 oz) plain flour
25 g (1 oz) cornflour
25 g (1 oz) cocoa
2 tsp baking powder
pinch of salt
2 eggs
150 g (5 oz) caster sugar
5 tbsp corn oil
5 tbsp water

Lightly oil and base-line two 15-cm (6-inch) sandwich tins and oil the lining paper. Heat the oven to 180°C (350°F) mark 4.

Sieve the flour, cornflour, cocoa, baking powder and salt into a mixing bowl. Separate the eggs then whisk the yolks with the sugar, oil and water and stir into the sieved ingredients, mixing well until evenly blended. Whisk the egg whites until they form stiff peaks, then fold lightly into the mixture. Place in the prepared tins, dividing the mixture equally between them; smooth over the top and bake for 25-30 minutes or until firm to the touch and beginning to shrink from the sides of the tin. Allow to cool in the tin for 3-4 minutes then turn out onto a cooling rack.

When cold, sandwich together with the chosen filling (see chapter 6) and dust with icing sugar.

WHOLEWHEAT FRUIT CAKE

100 g (4 oz) currants
100 g (4 oz) sultanas or raisins
100 g (4 oz) margarine
175 g (6 oz) soft brown sugar
50 g (2 oz) chopped mixed peel
25 g (1 oz) chopped glacé cherries
225 ml (8 fl oz) water
1 tsp bicarbonate of soda
2 tsp mixed spice
1 tsp ground nutmeg
225 g (8 oz) wholemeal flour
1 tsp baking powder
pinch of salt
2 eggs

Heat the oven to 180°C (350°F) mark 4. Lightly grease and line an 18-cm (7-inch) square cake tin and lightly grease the lining paper.

Wash the dried fruit and place in a saucepan with the margarine, sugar, peel, cherries, water, bicarbonate of soda and spices. Bring to the boil and simmer gently for 1 minute. Pour into a large mixing bowl and allow to cool.

Sieve the flour with the baking powder and salt, adding the residue in the sieve to the flour, then stir into the melted mixture together with the lightly beaten eggs. Mix well, then place in the prepared tin, smoothing over the top.

Bake for 1¼-1½ hours or until golden in colour, firm to the touch and beginning to shrink from the sides of the tin. Allow to cool in the tin for 15 minutes then turn out onto a cooling rack.

PARKIN

175 g (6 oz) wholemeal flour
175 g (6 oz) medium oatmeal
2 tsp ground ginger
1 tsp ground cinnamon
¼ tsp ground nutmeg
100 g (4 oz) margarine
75 g (3 oz) soft brown sugar
100 g (4 oz) black treacle
175 g (6 oz) golden syrup
1 egg
1 tsp bicarbonate of soda
150 ml (¼ pint) milk

Heat the oven to 150°C (300°F) mark 2. Lightly grease and line an oblong tin, about 28 × 18 × 4 cm (11 × 7 × 1½ inches) and lightly grease the lining paper.

Place the flour, oatmeal, ginger, cinnamon and nutmeg in a mixing bowl and mix well. Place the margarine, sugar, treacle and syrup in a small saucepan and place over a gentle heat until the margarine has melted and the sugar is dissolved; mix into the dry ingredients. Beat the egg, dissolve the bicarbonate of soda in a little of the milk and mix with the egg into the flour and fat mixture. Add sufficient milk to give the consistency of batter.

Place in the prepared tin, spreading well into the corners, and bake for about 1 hour or until firm to the touch and beginning to shrink from the sides of the tin. Allow to cool in the tin until quite cold, then, turn out and remove the lining paper.

Wrap in greaseproof paper and store for about a week, after which the parkin will be moist and almost sticky. Cut into pieces.

SHEARERS CAKE

400 g (14 oz) mixed dried fruit
225 g (8 oz) margarine
350 g (12 oz) granulated sugar
350 ml (12 fl oz) water
1 tsp bicarbonate of soda
275 g (10 oz) plain wholemeal flour
275 g (10 oz) self-raising flour
1-2 tbsp milk

Heat the oven to 150°C (300°F) mark 2. Lightly grease and line a 20-cm (8-inch) round cake tin and lightly grease the lining paper. Wash and dry the dried fruit.

Place the margarine, sugar, water, dried fruit and bicarbonate of soda in a saucepan. Heat gently to dissolve the margarine then bring to the boil, stirring to dissolve the sugar. Simmer for 3 minutes then allow to cool until tepid. Meanwhile, mix the flours together then add the tepid mixture and beat well until thoroughly mixed. Add the milk.

Place in the prepared tin and bake for about 2 hours or until firm to the touch and beginning to shrink from the sides of the tin. Allow to cool in the tin for 10 minutes, then turn out onto a cooling rack and remove the lining paper.

This is an old Scottish recipe.

ONE-STAGE SANDWICH CAKE

175 g (6 oz) self-raising flour
pinch of salt
1½ tsp baking powder
3 large eggs
175 g (6 oz) soft margarine
175 g (6 oz) caster sugar

Heat the oven to 170°C (325°F) mark 3. Lightly grease and line the base of two 18-cm (7-inch) sandwich cake tins and lightly grease the lining paper.

Sieve the flour, salt and baking powder into a mixing bowl, add the remaining ingredients and beat well for 2-3 minutes until evenly blended. Divide equally between the tins and hollow out the centre a little.

Bake for 25-30 minutes or until firm to the touch and beginning to shrink from the sides of the tin. Allow to cool in the tin for 3-4 minutes then turn out onto a cooling rack. Fill as desired.

Variations

(1) Chocolate: substitute 2 tablespoonfuls cocoa powder for 2 tablespoonfuls flour; add a few drops of vanilla flavouring. Sandwich together with vanilla, chocolate or coffee butter cream (see page 90); dredge lightly with sieved icing sugar before serving.

(2) Coffee: add 1 tablespoonful coffee essence to the mixture. Sandwich together with coffee butter cream (see page 90). Dredge lightly with sieved icing sugar before serving.

(3) Lemon: add the finely grated zest of 1 lemon plus 1 tablespoonful lemon juice to the mixture. Sandwich together with lemon-flavoured butter cream (see page 90) or lemon curd. Dust lightly with caster sugar before serving.

(5) Victoria: add a few drops of vanilla flavouring to the mixture and sandwich together with raspberry jam. Dust lightly with caster sugar before serving.

SANDWICH CAKES

150 g (5 oz) self-raising flour
1 tsp baking powder
pinch of salt
115 g (4½ oz) caster sugar
7 tbsp corn oil
2 eggs
2½ tbsp milk
½ tsp vanilla flavouring

Frosting (using oil)
100 g (4 oz) icing sugar
2 tbsp corn oil
1½-2 tbsp milk
½ tsp vanilla flavouring

Heat the oven to 180°C (350°F) mark 4. Lightly oil two 18-cm (7-inch) sandwich tins and line the base with greaseproof paper. Lightly oil the lining paper.

Sieve the flour with the baking powder and salt; stir in the sugar. Add the oil, the lightly beaten eggs, the milk and vanilla flavouring and beat thoroughly until completely blended. Divide the mixture evenly between the prepared tins and bake for about 25-30 minutes or until firm to the touch and beginning to shrink from the sides of the tins. Allow to cool in the tins for 3-4 minutes then turn out onto a cooling rack. When cold fill with chosen filling (see chapter 6).

For the frosting, sieve the icing sugar, then beat in the remaining ingredients until a smooth frosting is formed. Use to top the cake or, if preferred, simply dust the cake with a little caster sugar or icing sugar before serving.

Variations

(1) Chocolate cake: substitute 1 tablespoonful cocoa for 1 tablespoonful flour. For the frosting, substitute 1 tablespoonful cocoa for 1 tablespoonful icing sugar but mix the cocoa with the milk which has been warmed.

(2) Coffee cake: add 2 teaspoonfuls coffee essence to the cake mixture and add 2 teaspoonfuls coffee essence to the frosting mixture.

(3) Lemon or orange cake: add the finely grated zest of 1 orange or lemon to the cake mixture. For the frosting, mix with 1½-2 tablespoonfuls orange or lemon juice instead of the milk, then tint lightly.

CHOCOLATE ORANGE CAKE

100 g (4 oz) self-raising flour
1 tsp baking powder
25 g (1 oz) cocoa
100 g (4 oz) soft margarine
150 g (5 oz) caster sugar
25 g (1 oz) golden syrup
2 eggs
50 g (2 oz) plain chocolate
finely grated zest and juice of 1 orange

Heat the oven to 180°C (350°F) mark 4. Lightly grease and line an 18-cm (7-inch) round cake tin and grease the lining paper.

Sieve the flour, baking powder and cocoa into a mixing bowl. Add all the remaining ingredients except the chocolate, orange zest and juice. Beat the mixture for about 3-4 minutes or until well blended. Grate the chocolate into the bowl and mix in together with the orange zest and juice.

Place in the prepared tin and smooth over the top. Mix the topping ingredients together

Topping
25 g (1 oz) soft brown sugar
25 g (1 oz) chopped walnuts

and sprinkle over the cake mixture. Bake for 30 minutes then reduce the oven temperature to 170°C (325°F) mark 3 and cook for a further 15-25 minutes or until firm to the touch and beginning to shrink from the sides of the tin.

Allow to cool in the tin for 10 minutes then turn out onto a cooling rack.

DATE SQUARES

225 g (8 oz) dates
finely grated zest and juice of 1 orange
175 g (6 oz) rolled oats
100 g (4 oz) plain flour
175 g (6 oz) soft brown sugar
175 g (6 oz) margarine

Heat the oven to 180°C (350°F) mark 4. Lightly grease and line a shallow 18-cm (7-inch) square tin and grease the lining paper.

Chop the dates and place in a small saucepan with the orange zest. Make up the orange juice to 150 ml (¼ pint) with water and add to the pan. Cook over a low heat, stirring continuously, until thick and the dates are softened. Leave to cool.

Mix the rolled oats, the flour and the sugar together; melt the margarine and mix in with a fork to give a crumbly texture. Press half the mixture into the tin, cover with the cooled date mixture, then top with the remaining crumb mixture. Press down lightly.

Bake for about 30 minutes or until golden brown and firm to the touch. Allow to cool in the tin then cut into squares or fingers. Place on a cooling rack.

GINGERBREAD

225 g (8 oz) margarine
225 g (8 oz) soft brown sugar
225 g (8 oz) black treacle
2 eggs
350 g (12 oz) plain flour
4 tsp ground ginger
3 tsp ground cinnamon
pinch of salt
275 ml (½ pint) milk
2 tsp bicarbonate of soda

Heat the oven to 150°C (300°F) mark 2. Lightly grease and line an 18 × 29-cm (7 × 11½-inch) shallow oblong tin (e.g. a roasting tin) and grease the lining paper.

Place the margarine, sugar and treacle in a saucepan and heat very gently until the sugar dissolves (do not boil or the gingerbread will be hard). Leave to cool. Lightly beat the eggs and stir into the cooled, melted mixture.

Sieve together the flour, the spices and salt. Stir into the melted mixture, making sure they are thoroughly blended. Warm the milk to blood heat and stir in the bicarbonate of soda. Add to the mixture, blending in thoroughly. Pour the mixture into the prepared tin.

Bake for about 1½ hours or until firm to the touch and beginning to shrink from the sides of the tin (it may be necessary to cover with a sheet of foil after 1 hour).

Allow to cool in the tin before turning out onto a cooling rack.

Gingerbread is best if wrapped in greaseproof paper or foil for 3-4 days before eating, then it will be moist and sticky.

Variations

(1) Substitute wholemeal flour for white flour, adding an extra tablespoonful of milk.
(2) Add the finely grated zest of 1 orange.
(3) Add 50 g (2 oz) sultanas or raisins.
(4) Add 50 g (2 oz) chopped, preserved ginger.

ORANGE AND RAISIN WHEATMEAL CAKE

50 g (2 oz) raisins
175 g (6 oz) self-raising flour
½ tsp bicarbonate of soda
pinch of salt
175 g (6 oz) wholemeal flour
finely grated zest of 1 orange
3 eggs
200 ml (7 fl oz) corn oil
4 tbsp orange marmalade
175 g (6 oz) soft brown sugar
4 tbsp milk

Heat the oven to 170°C (325°F) mark 3. Lightly oil and line an 18-cm (7-inch) square or 20-cm (8-inch) round cake tin and lightly oil the lining paper.

Wash the raisins and dry thoroughly. Sieve the self-raising flour with the bicarbonate of soda and salt and stir in the wholemeal flour. Add the prepared fruit and orange zest and mix well. Whisk the eggs, then mix with the oil, marmalade, sugar and milk, blending well. Stir into the dry mixture and beat well until evenly blended.

Place in the prepared tin and bake for 1½-1¾ hours or until firm to the touch and beginning to shrink from the sides of the tin.

Allow to cool in the tin for 10 minutes then turn out onto a cooling rack and remove the lining paper.

DANISH APPLE CAKE

225 g (8 oz) plain flour
½ tsp baking powder
¼ tsp salt
100 g (4 oz) margarine
100 g (4 oz) soft brown sugar
1 egg
a little icing sugar to dredge

Apple filling
350 g (12 oz) cooking apples
50 g (2 oz) raisins
1 tbsp dark soft brown sugar
½ tsp ground cinnamon or ground ginger

Heat the oven to 180°C (350°F) mark 4. Lightly grease and line a 20-cm (8-inch) shallow, square cake tin and lightly grease the lining paper.

Peel, core and slice the apples thinly. Sieve the flour with the baking powder and salt. Wash the raisins and dry thoroughly.

Melt the margarine and mix with the sugar; add the lightly beaten egg and mix well. Gradually mix in the sieved flour mixture. Spread two thirds of the cake mixture over the base of the prepared tin. Place the apples and raisins over the mixture and sprinkle with the soft brown sugar and the cinnamon or ginger. Place the remainder of the cake mixture in spoonfuls on top.

Bake for 40-45 minutes or until golden, firm to the touch and beginning to shrink from the sides of the tin. Allow to cool in the tin for 15 minutes then turn out onto a cooling rack. Serve sprinkled with sieved icing sugar.

PINEAPPLE CAKE

425 g (15 oz) canned pineapple
100 g (4 oz) glacé cherries
100 g (4 oz) self-raising flour
100 g (4 oz) plain flour
pinch of salt
225 g (8 oz) sultanas
100 g (4 oz) margarine
100 g (4 oz) soft brown sugar
100 g (4 oz) chopped dates
1 tsp bicarbonate of soda
2 eggs
1 tsp vanilla flavouring

Heat the oven to 180°C (350°F) mark 4. Lightly grease and line a 20-cm (8-inch) round cake tin and lightly grease the lining paper. Drain the pineapple and chop, retaining the juice. Quarter the cherries and sieve the flours with the salt. Wash and dry the sultanas.

Simmer together the pineapple, pineapple juice, margarine, sugar, sultanas, cherries and dates for 15 minutes. Add the bicarbonate of soda and allow the mixture to cool. Fold in the sieved flour together with the beaten eggs and vanilla flavouring.

Place in the prepared tin, smooth over the top and bake for 45 minutes then reduce the oven temperature to 170°C (325°F) mark 3 for a further 30-45 minutes or until golden in colour, firm to the touch and beginning to shrink from the sides of the tin. Allow to cool in the tin for 15 minutes then turn out onto a cooling rack.

CHERRY AND ORANGE LOAF

275 g (10 oz) self-raising flour
pinch of salt
175 g (6 oz) glacé cherries
120 ml (4 fl oz) vegetable oil
2 eggs
2 tbsp milk
150 g (5 oz) caster sugar
zest of ½ orange

Heat the oven to 180°C (350°F) mark 4. Lightly grease an 18-cm (7-inch) round cake tin or a 900-g (2-lb) loaf tin. Sieve the flour and salt; quarter the cherries.

Place the oil, eggs, milk and sugar together in a mixing bowl and whisk until evenly blended. Fold in the flour evenly then fold in the cherries and orange zest.

Place in the prepared tin, smooth over the top and bake for about 1 hour until golden in colour, firm to the touch and beginning to shrink from the sides of the tin.

Allow to cool in the tin for 7-8 minutes then turn out onto a cooling rack. Remove the lining paper.

Variation

You can successfully substitute honey for the caster sugar and wholemeal self-raising flour for white flour, though it may be necessary to add an extra tablespoonful milk as wholemeal flour absorbs more liquid.

MICROWAVE CAKES

This chapter includes a small number of cake recipes suitable for a microwave oven. Remember to check the manufacturer's instructions before starting.

These cakes have been tested in a microwave oven with a 650 watt output. Some microwave ovens have a higher output, in which case it will be necessary to check carefully to avoid overcooking.

The recipe book which comes with your microwave will give guidance on testing whether the cake is sufficiently cooked. Wave patterns vary in different ovens so it may be necessary to rotate cooking containers once or twice during cooking to get an even rise.

Tests for whether a cake is cooked are similar to those used when baking in a conventional oven: it is ready when firm to the touch and beginning to shrink from the sides of the container.

SMALL CAKES

Makes 36

175 g (6 oz) margarine
175 g (6 oz) caster sugar
3 eggs
175 g (6 oz) self-raising flour
1 tbsp hot water

Using a basic 3-egg creamed mixture (see page 48 for method) a wide variety of small cakes may be made in the microwave oven. By dividing the basic mixture into four sections and adding chosen flavourings, 36 small cakes, suitable for icing, can be cooked in about 6 minutes.

Suggestions for flavourings

(1) To a quarter of the mixture add 1 teaspoonful cocoa blended with 2 teaspoonfuls milk plus a few drops of vanilla flavouring.

(2) To a quarter of the mixture add 2 teaspoonfuls orange juice and a little finely grated orange zest.

(3) To a quarter of the mixture add 1 teaspoonful coffee essence.
(4) To a quarter of the mixture add a few drops of green food colouring and a few drops of almond essence or peppermint essence.
(5) To add variety, use a teaspoonful of any two of the above flavoured mixtures in each paper case and swirl the two mixtures together with the blade of a knife, before baking.

Use double thickness paper cake cases no more than half full of cake mixture.

Arrange up to 10 filled cases in a circle, allowing a little space between each one. If using an oven with a turntable, space the paper cases around the edge of the turntable. Cook on High for about 2 minutes or until just set in the centre. Remove from the oven and allow to stand for 3-4 minutes. Repeat with the remaining filled paper cases.

If cooking fewer than 10 cakes, the cooking time will be shorter.

Ice with flavoured glacé icing (see page 86) or butter cream (see page 90). Decorate as desired.

ORANGE GINGERBREAD

100 g (4 oz) margarine
100 g (4 oz) soft brown sugar
6 tbsp golden syrup
6 tbsp black treacle
100 g (4 oz) plain flour
1 tsp bicarbonate of soda
2 tsp mixed spice
3 tsp ground ginger

Use a large, shallow dish suitable for use in a microwave oven, for example an oblong casserole, an oven-glass roaster etc., about 2.4-litre (4-pint) capacity. Lightly grease or oil and line the base with greaseproof paper; grease this lining paper.

Place the margarine, sugar, syrup and treacle in a mixing bowl and place in the

½ tsp salt
100 g (4 oz) wholemeal flour
2 eggs
4 tbsp milk
finely grated zest of 2 oranges
juice of 1 orange

microwave oven. Cook on High for about 2 minutes or until the margarine has melted. Sieve the plain flour with the bicarbonate of soda, spices and salt then stir in the wholemeal flour. Lightly beat the eggs with the milk.

Mix all the ingredients together, adding the orange zest and juice. Mix thoroughly then place in the prepared container. If using an oblong dish, protect the corners from overcooking by pressing a small piece of foil across each corner, securing the foil under the rim of the dish.

The gingerbread batter should half-fill the container; if there is more than this, bake the remaining batter either in double thickness paper cases or in a small dish.

Cook for about 8-9 minutes on High or until just set in the centre. It is better to undercook, as extra cooking time can always be added. Test any moist spots on the surface by touching lightly with your finger: if the moisture comes off on your finger leaving the surface dry, the cake is done. To ensure even rising, it is advisable to rotate the container three or four times during cooking, removing the foil protection for the last 3-4 minutes of cooking.

Allow the gingerbread to stand in its container on a working surface for 5 minutes before turning out.

CHOCOLATE ORANGE YOGHURT CAKE

225 g (8 oz) self-raising flour
5 tbsp cocoa
pinch of salt
1/2 tsp bicarbonate of soda
3 eggs
150 ml (1/4 pint) sunflower or corn oil
150 ml (1/4 pint) orange-flavoured yoghurt
4 tbsp golden syrup
175 g (6 oz) soft brown sugar
finely grated zest of 1 orange

Topping (optional)
fudge icing (see page 87) or quick frosting (see page 89)

Use a suitable container like a straight-sided soufflé dish (without any metal trim), a straight-sided casserole dish, a microware cake baker, a microware ring mould etc., with a liquid capacity of 2.4 litres (4 pints). Oil or lightly grease the dish and line the base with greaseproof paper; oil or grease the lining.

Prepare the mixture (see method page 59) and place in the prepared dish, making sure the dish is not more than half full. Any additional mixture can be cooked either in double thickness paper cases or in a small dish.

Cook on High for about 9 minutes, rotating the dish three to four times during cooking to ensure an even rise. When cooked, the cake should be just set in the centre. Allow to stand on a working surface for 5 minutes, then turn out. Finish with frosting as for the cake cooked by the traditional method (see page 59).

SANDWICH CAKES

175 g (6 oz) margarine
175 g (6 oz) caster sugar
3 eggs
175 g (6 oz) self-raising flour
a few drops of vanilla flavouring
1 tbsp hot water

Using a basic 3-egg creamed mixture (see page 48 for method), various flavoured sandwich cakes may be cooked in the microwave oven. A better finish can be obtained if the sides of the sandwich cake are also iced and decorated.

For containers, use a microware 18-cm (7-inch) cake dish with a capacity of 1.75 litres (3 pints), or a straight-sided 18-cm (7-inch) soufflé dish. Lightly grease the chosen dish and line the base with greaseproof paper; lightly grease the paper.

Divide the mixture in half, place half in the prepared container or, if preferred, the whole mixture can be cooked together and cut in half when cold.

Microwave on High for about 4 minutes if using half the mixture, or on High for about 6-7 minutes if using the whole mixture.

ICINGS AND FILLINGS

This chapter includes recipes for very simple water icings, frostings and butter creams as well as some recipes for slightly more advanced icings. There are also recipes for making and applying the traditional almond paste and Royal icings for seasonal special occasion cakes.

ALMOND PASTE

Sufficient to cover the top and sides of an 18-cm (7-inch) round cake or a 15-cm (6-inch) square cake

225 g (8 oz) ground almonds
100 g (4 oz) sieved icing sugar
100 g (4 oz) caster sugar
1 tsp lemon juice
a few drops of almond essence
a few drops of vanilla flavouring
1 egg

Place the dry ingredients in a mixing bowl, make a well in the centre and add the flavourings together with sufficient beaten egg to give a firm consistency. Knead very lightly to remove any cracks but avoid over-handling as the paste could become oily and will be difficult to handle. Wrap in clingfilm or a polythene bag to prevent the paste drying out.

Almond paste adds flavour and richness to the cake, as well as providing a smooth, protective layer between the cake and the final coat of Royal icing. If almond paste is not used, it is difficult to achieve an even finish with Royal icing and there is a tendency for the Royal icing to discolour.

Almond paste can also be used to shape small petits fours and with the addition of a little food colouring, a selection of small fruits can be modelled.

To prevent almond paste drying out, it is necessary to closely wrap it in clingfilm. It can be stored, in a plastic bag, in the refrigerator for two to three weeks.

required amount of almond paste (see chart overleaf)
apricot glaze (see page 93)

To apply almond paste
Using the cake tin in which the cake was made, cut out a circle or square of greaseproof paper the same size as the base of the tin. Warm the apricot glaze.

Using one third of the almond paste, dust a working surface *very lightly* with cornflour and roll out the paste to a circle the same size as the paper pattern (alternatively roll out the paste on the greaseproof pattern).

Brush the top of the cake with apricot glaze and invert onto the almond paste so that the two surfaces are joined. Using a palette knife, press the edge of the almond paste to the edge of the cake. Place the cake

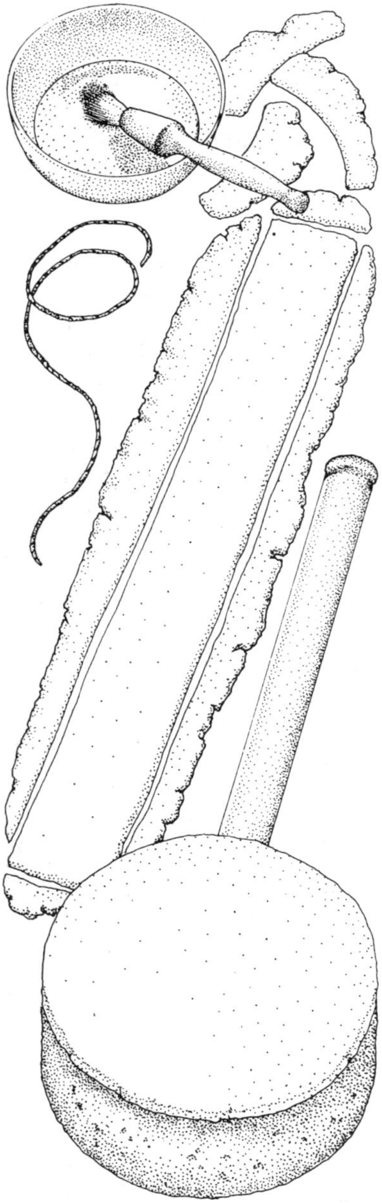

the right way up.

Using the remaining two thirds of the almond paste, for a *round* cake, measure the exact circumference of the cake with a piece of string. Cut the string to this measurement. Using the same piece of string, measure the depth of the cake and mark this on the string.

Roll out the almond paste on a working surface very lightly dusted with cornflour. Roll to a strip of about the same size as the string (the length equal to the circumference and the width equal to the depth). Using the string, measure the exact length and trim the ends square. Trim one long edge of the almond paste, then, using the depth measurement of the string, measure from this trimmed edge to the opposite edge and make a series of guide marks all along its length. Trim this edge.

Brush the strip of almond paste with the warmed apricot glaze and check that it is not sticking to the working surface by sliding a palette knife under the paste.

Holding the cake on its edge (with its top already covered with the paste) as if it were a wheel, place the two edges of the almond paste together, ensuring a good sharp edge. Roll the cake along the strip of almond paste, keeping the edges level, until the cake is completely covered. It may be necessary to trim the final edge of the paste.

Place the cake the right way up and, using a small palette knife, gently smooth the joins to give an even finish. Using a straight-sided jam jar, roll this lightly around the side of the cake to ensure a straight edge. Finally, using a rolling pin, lightly roll the top of the cake.

For a *square* cake, cover the top of the cake in the same way as for the round cake. Using string, measure the length and depth of one side of the cake. Roll out a quarter of the remaining paste to this measurement and trim and apply to the cake in the same way as for the round cake. Measure each remaining side separately to find its size.

Complete as for the round cake. Store the cake, uncovered, in a warm, well-ventilated place, for 2-3 days or until the icing becomes matt in finish. Failure to do this could result in the final coat of Royal icing turning yellow from the oil in the almonds.

Quantities of almond paste to cover the top and sides of rich fruit cakes

Square	12.5-cm (5-inch)	15-cm (6-inch)	18-cm (7-inch)	20-cm (8-inch)	23-cm (9-inch)	25-cm (10-inch)
Round	15-cm (6-inch)	18-cm (7-inch)	20-cm (8-inch)	23-cm (9-inch)	25-cm (10-inch)	28-cm (11-inch)
Ground almonds	175 g (6 oz)	225 g (8 oz)	350 g (12 oz)	450 g (1 lb)	575 g (1¼ lb)	675 g (1½ lb)
Caster sugar	75 g (3 oz)	100 g (4 oz)	175 g (6 oz)	225 g (8 oz)	275 g (10 oz)	350 g (12 oz)
Icing sugar	75 g (3 oz)	100 g (4 oz)	175 g (6 oz)	225 g (8 oz)	275 g (10 oz)	350 g (12 oz)
Lemon juice	1 tsp	1 tsp	2 tsp	2 tsp	3 tsp	3 tsp
Almond essence	a few drops	a few drops	a few drops	a few drops	¼ tsp	¼ tsp
Vanilla flavouring	a few drops	a few drops	a few drops	a few drops	¼ tsp	¼ tsp
Eggs	½-¾	1	1	1 large	2½	3 large

ROYAL ICING

Sufficient to cover the top and sides of a 15-cm (6-inch) square cake or an 18-cm (7-inch) round cake

2 egg whites
450 g (1 lb) sieved icing sugar
1 tsp glycerine
a little lemon juice (optional)

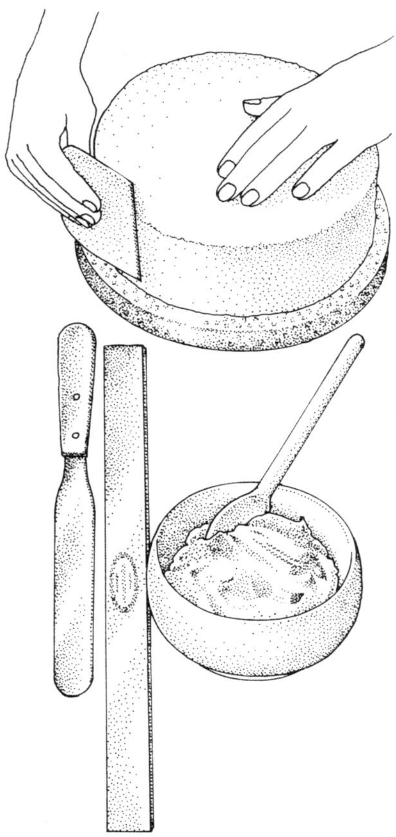

Place the egg whites in a mixing bowl and whisk lightly with a fork until just frothy. Add the sieved icing sugar, a tablespoonful at a time, beating well between each addition until the icing is smooth and white. Add the glycerine and lemon juice (if used). The consistency will be thick enough to just hold its shape. Cover the icing with a damp cloth or clingfilm and allow to stand for 3-4 hours to allow any bubbles to rise to the surface and burst.

To ice the top and sides of an almond-pasted cake

Choose a cake board which is at least 1½-2 inches larger than the cake.

Spread a little icing in the centre of the board and position the cake in the centre. Place the board with the cake on a turntable or an upturned plate.

Mix the icing lightly to allow the bubbles to come to the surface and burst as many as possible using a palette knife.

Place about half the icing on top of the cake and spread firmly to the edges using a palette knife (firm pressure will burst any other bubbles). When the icing is evenly spread, draw a metal rule or icing ruler across the top of the cake, working towards you and holding the rule at a slight angle. Try to do this as lightly as possible, just to make the icing smooth. Remove any surplus icing at the edge of the cake, holding a palette knife parallel with the side of the cake. Leave the icing to dry out.

For the side of a round cake, spread a thin layer of icing to cover the side of the cake, making it as smooth as possible. Using a plastic icing scraper held at an angle of 45° to the cake and starting furthest away from you

– i.e. at the back of the cake – rotate the cake with your other hand, in one movement, so that the side of the cake is smoothed by the plastic scraper. Remove any surplus on the top edge and the base with a palette knife. Allow to dry out.

For a square cake, it is better to ice opposite sides first, allowing this icing to dry out before icing the remaining sides.

For subsequent coatings, allow the first coat to dry out beforehand. For a very smooth finish, remove any small rough edges with a very sharp knife, then rub over with a fine sandpaper.

To ice the cake board, spread a thin layer of icing on the board, keeping it as smooth as possible. Remove any surplus, holding either a palette knife or an icing scraper at an angle and rotating the turntable. Remove any surplus from the edge of the board. Allow it to dry out, then decorate as desired.

Quantities required to ice the top and sides of rich fruit cakes

Square	12.5-cm (5-inch)	15-cm (6-inch)	18-cm (7-inch)	20-cm (8-inch)	23-cm (9-inch)	25-cm (10-inch)
Round	15-cm (6-inch)	18-cm (7-inch)	20-cm (8-inch)	23-cm (9-inch)	25-cm (10-inch)	28-cm (11-inch)
Egg whites	2	2	3	3	4	4
Icing sugar	450 g (1 lb)	450 g (1 lb)	675 g (1½ lb)	675 g (1½ lb)	900 g (2 lb)	900 g (2 lb)
Lemon juice	a few drops	a few drops	a few drops	a few drops	a few drops	a few drops
Glycerine	1 tsp	1 tsp	1½ tsp	1½ tsp	2 tsp	2 tsp

ROYAL ICING (FLOW-COATING)

Sufficient to coat the top and sides of a 15-cm (6-inch) square cake or an 18-cm (7-inch) round cake

3-4 egg whites
450 g (1 lb) sieved icing sugar
2-3 tsp glycerine

Lightly whisk 2 of the egg whites in a roomy mixing bowl. Work in about half the sieved icing sugar and beat vigorously until the icing loses its slight yellow tinge. Work in the remaining sugar together with the glycerine, adding sufficient egg white to give a soft consistency which will thickly coat the back of a wooden spoon and will slowly settle to its own level in the mixing bowl.

Cover with clingfilm and allow to stand for 24 hours to allow air bubbles to rise to the surface. Burst as many air bubbles as possible, occasionally giving the bowl a firm bump to allow more bubbles to surface.

This icing can be run onto the prepared cake in the same manner as glacé icing.

GLACÉ ICING

Sufficient to cover the top of an 18-cm (7-inch) cake

175 g (6 oz) icing sugar
2-3 tbsp hot water or stock syrup (*see page 93*)
½ tsp lemon juice (optional)

Sieve the icing sugar into a mixing bowl; make a well in the centre and gradually beat in the water or stock syrup. Add flavouring, if used (see Variations). Beat the icing well, adding sieved icing sugar or liquid to achieve a consistency which will smoothly coat the back of a wooden spoon and just find its own level in the mixing bowl. Use at once or cover with plastic film to prevent the icing from setting. Add any chosen food colouring.

Variations

(1) Coffee: add 1-2 teaspoonfuls coffee essence in place of the same quantity of water.

(2) Chocolate: blend 2 tablespoonfuls cocoa with 2 tablespoonfuls hot water or stock syrup. Cool, then add to the other ingredients, substituting a few drops of

vanilla flavouring for the lemon juice. The addition of 1 small teaspoonful corn oil or 1 tablespoonful apricot glaze (see page 93) will give this icing a good sheen.

FUDGE ICING

Sufficient to ice and fill an 18-cm (7-inch) sandwich cake

50 g (2 oz) butter or margarine
225 g (8 oz) icing sugar
3 tbsp milk

Place the ingredients in a heat-resistant bowl and place over a pan of gently steaming water. Stir well to blend and continue until the icing is smooth. Remove from the heat and allow to cool. When the icing is almost cold, beat well until it thickens to a spreading consistency. This icing can be used as a filling as well as an icing.

Alternatively, the icing can be used while still lukewarm, when it can be poured over the cake and allowed to set.

Variations

(1) Coffee: substitute 1 tablespoonful coffee essence for 1 tablespoonful milk or dissolve 1 teaspoonful instant coffee in the mixture in the bowl.

(2) Chocolate: sieve 2 tablespoonfuls cocoa with the icing sugar and add a few drops of vanilla flavouring.

(3) Mocha: sieve 1 tablespoonful cocoa with the icing sugar and substitute 1 tablespoonful coffee essence for 1 tablespoonful milk as in the coffee fudge icing.

MOCK FONDANT ICING

Sufficient to cover the top and sides of a 15-cm (6-inch) square or an 18-cm (7-inch) round cake

1 egg white
1 heaped tbsp liquid glucose
450 g (1 lb) sieved icing sugar

Place the egg white and liquid glucose in a mixing bowl and stir together to mix. Add 225 g (8 oz) of the sieved icing sugar and mix well. Gradually add some of the remaining icing sugar until the icing becomes fairly stiff, then knead in the remainder. Turn out on to a working surface and knead firmly to form a smooth, silky paste. Use at once or wrap in clingfilm and keep in a plastic bag in the refrigerator.

To ice a cake with mock fondant icing
Knead the icing until it becomes pliable and soft to handle. Lightly dust a working surface with cornflour and roll out the icing until it is about 5 cm (2 inches) larger than the top of the cake.

Carefully lift the icing and place on top of the cake (it is sometimes easier to lift the icing on a rolling pin as when lining a flan ring). Dust your hands with cornflour and lightly press the icing onto the cake, moulding it into position down the sides. Gentle moulding, using your hands dusted with cornflour, will give a sheen and an even coating.

Trim the icing at the bottom of the cake. This icing may be decorated immediately, if desired.

Wrap any trimmings in clingfilm and place in a polythene bag in the refrigerator. These trimmings may be tinted with food colouring and used for making decorations.

This is a quickly made icing which is easy to handle and can be used to cover the top and sides of cakes. It is also very useful for making decorations for cakes.

QUICK SEVEN-MINUTE FROSTING

Sufficient to coat a 20-cm (8-inch) cake

175 g (6 oz) caster sugar
2 tbsp cold water
very scant 1/4 tsp cream of tartar
1 unbeaten egg white

Place the sugar with the water in a heat-resistant bowl; stir to partially dissolve the sugar then add the remaining ingredients. Place the bowl over a pan of gently simmering water and whisk until the frosting thickens and the mixture will hold a stiff peak when the whisk is removed.

Remove the bowl from the heat and spoon over the cake *at once* as this frosting sets very quickly. Use a palette knife or spoon to pull the icing into peaks, if desired.

This is a quicker version of the traditional American frosting.

PRALINE

50 g (2 oz) caster sugar
50 g (2 oz) unblanched almonds

Lightly oil a heavy baking sheet. Place the sugar and almonds in a small, heavy-based saucepan and place over a gentle heat to dissolve the sugar into a colourless liquid. When the sugar is completely dissolved, raise the heat slightly and, *without stirring*, continue to cook until the sugar becomes a good hazelnut brown.

Pour at once onto the prepared baking sheet. Allow to become cold, then loosen from the baking sheet. Break into pieces and either crush between two sheets of greaseproof paper or place in a food processor or blender and grind to a powder. Care should be taken to avoid over-processing or blending, as the mixture could become a paste. Store in an airtight container.

BUTTER CREAM

Sufficient to fill and ice the top of a 20-cm (8-inch) cake

100 g (4 oz) butter or margarine
225 g (8 oz) sieved icing sugar
1-2 tbsp milk

Place the butter or margarine in a mixing bowl and beat well to soften. Add the icing sugar, a little at a time, beating well. Add sufficient milk to give a consistency which will stand in soft peaks. Spread as a filling or as a covering for light, textured cakes. This cream can also be used to decorate with a piped design.

Variations
(1) Chocolate: blend 2 rounded tablespoonfuls cocoa with 2 tablespoonfuls hot water; when cooled, beat into the butter cream before adding the milk. Add only suficient milk to give the correct consistency.
(2) Coffee: add 1 tablespoonful coffee essence, adjusting the amount of milk as in chocolate cream (above).
(3) Lemon or orange: add the finely grated zest of ½-1 lemon or orange and substitute 1 tablespoonful lemon or orange juice for 1 tablespoonful milk. Tint with food colouring if desired.
(4) Peppermint: add a few drops of peppermint oil or essence and tint, very sparingly, with green food colouring.
(5) Vanilla: add a few drops of vanilla flavouring.

CRÈME AU BEURRE

Sufficient to coat the top and sides of an 18-cm (7-inch) cake

65 g (2½ oz) granulated sugar
4 tbsp water
2 egg yolks
150 g (5 oz) unsalted butter

Place the sugar with the water in a small, heavy-based saucepan. Place over a low heat and allow the sugar to dissolve completely, stirring occasionally. Meanwhile, beat the egg yolks lightly in a heat-resistant bowl.

Bring the sugar mixture to the boil and *without stirring* boil until it reaches a temperature of 104°C (218°F) or until the mixture will form a thread. Pour at once onto the egg yolks in a steady stream, beating or whisking well. Continue whisking until the mixture thickens and has a mousse-like consistency and is nearly cold.

Cream the butter until softened and beat in the egg and sugar mixture, a little at a time. Flavour as desired (see below).

If the mixture appears to curdle at any time during the beating or whisking, hold the bowl over hot water for a minute or two or add a little more butter.

To test for a thread without a sugar thermometer, remove the saucepan from the heat, dip a teaspoon in and coat it with the sugar syrup; allow the spoon to cool for a few seconds then touch the syrup with your finger. Lift your finger and you should see a thread of syrup forming between the spoon and your finger.

Variations

(1) Chocolate: add 100 g (4 oz) melted chocolate, beating in gradually.

(2) Coffee: beat in 1-2 tablespoonfuls coffee essence.

(3) Praline: beat 75-100 g (3-4 oz) powdered praline (see page 89) into the crème.

(4) Orange or lemon: add the finely grated zest of 1 orange or lemon.

(5) Rum: add 1-2 tablespoonfuls rum and beat well.

(6) Kirsch: add 2 tablespoonfuls kirsch and beat well.

CRÈME AU BEURRE À MERINGUE

Sufficient to fill and ice the top of a 20-cm (8-inch) cake

2 egg whites
100 g (4 oz) sieved icing sugar
225 g (8 oz) unsalted butter

Place the egg whites with the icing sugar in a heat-resistant mixing bowl and place over a saucepan of gently simmering water, ensuring that the base of the bowl is not touching the water. Whisk until the mixture just holds its shape when the whisk is lifted out. Remove from the heat and continue whisking until cooled and meringue-like.

Cream the butter until soft, then add the meringue, a little at a time, beating well between each addition.

Variations
As in crème au beurre (see page 90).

This crème is not as rich as that made with egg yolks, and because it is lighter in colour, is particularly good for tinting.

CARAMEL

100 g (4 oz) granulated or caster sugar
a little cooking oil

Lightly oil a heavy baking sheet. Place the sugar in a thick-based saucepan or in a strong, thick-based frying pan and place over a low heat. Allow the sugar to melt to a pale golden brown colour then pour immediately onto the prepared baking sheet. (It may be necessary to shake the saucepan or frying pan gently whilst the sugar is melting to ensure the sugar is evenly coloured, but avoid stirring as this could cause the sugar to crystallize).

The caramel will set rapidly and is easily removed from the baking sheet when cold.

The caramel may be broken into small pieces and used to decorate gâteaux or it may be crushed more finely and used to coat the sides of gâteaux in place of nuts.

APRICOT GLAZE

450 g (1 lb) apricot jam
4 tbsp water
1 tsp lemon juice

Place the jam and the water in a small, heavy-based saucepan; bring to the boil and cook for 4-5 minutes. Strain, then add the lemon juice. It may be necessary to boil up again to reach the required consistency – the glaze should just drop from the spoon when given a good shake.

The use of this glaze as a protective layer between the cake and the icing prevents any loose crumb being raised and mixed in with the icing. It is a good idea to make up the recipe and store, in a screw-topped jar, in the refrigerator.

The glaze is warmed, then brushed over the cake in a thin layer and allowed to set before the cake is iced.

The glaze is also used as a base for almond paste, as it helps the icing stick to the cake.

It can also be used as a glaze for fresh fruit in flans and gâteaux.

STOCK SYRUP

450 g (1 lb) granulated sugar
275 ml (½ pint) water

Place the sugar and water in a small, heavy-based saucepan; heat gently, stirring, until the sugar is dissolved, then bring to the boil and boil steadily, without stirring, until it reaches a temperature of 109°C (220°F). Strain into a heat-resistant jug, allow to cool, then transfer to a screw-topped jar for storage.

While glacé icing may be made quite successfully with hot water, stock syrup gives the finished icing a very good sheen. This syrup can be stored in the refrigerator for up to 2 weeks.

WHAT IS THE WI?

If you have enjoyed this book, the chances are that you would enjoy belonging to the largest women's organisation in the country – the Women's Institutes.

We are friendly, go-ahead, like-minded women, who derive enormous satisfaction from all the movement has to offer. This list is long – you can make new friends, have fun and companionship, visit new places, develop new skills, take part in community services, fight local campaigns, become a WI market producer, and play an active role in an organisation which has a national voice.

The WI is the only women's organisation in the country which owns an adult education establishment. At Denman College, you can take a course in anything from car maintenance to paper sculpture, from book-binding to yoga, or cordon bleu cookery to fly-fishing.

All you need to do to join is write to us here at the **National Federation of Women's Institutes, 39 Eccleston Street, London SW1W 9NT**, or telephone 01-730 7212, and we will put you in touch with WIs in your immediate locality. We hope to hear from you.

ABOUT THE AUTHOR

Lyn Mann is a trained home economics teacher: she has taught cookery in schools, technical colleges and at adult education classes. She recently retired as Head of the department of Rural Home Economics at the Berkshire College of Agriculture. A WI national cookery and preservation judge, demonstrator and assessor, Lyn belongs to Caversham WI and is a member of the Home Economics Sub-Committee of the Berkshire Federation of Women's Institutes.

INDEX